Winning Resources and Support

OU Business School

Book 6

Planning and Strategy

Prepared for the course team by Chris Cornforth, Jill Mordaunt and Terry O'Sullivan

COURSE TEAM

Dr Terry O'Sullivan, *Course Chair*

Barry Jones, *Course Manager*

Sue Treacy, *Course Team Assistant*

Sam Cooper, *OU Business School Regional Coordinator*

Joan Hunt, *OU Business School Regional Manager*

Amanda Shepard, *Institute of Fundraising*

Production Team

Simon Ashby, *Editor*

Paul Beeby, *Media Project Manager*

Martin Brazier, *Graphic Designer*

Holly Clements, *Picture research and Rights clearance*

Roy Lawrence, *Graphic Artist*

David Richings, *Materials procurement*

Critical Readers

Sam Cooper, *Programme Coordinator*

Gail Devlin-Jones, *Eranda Foundation*

Chris Durkin, *University of Northampton*

Acknowledgements

We are grateful to the Institute of Fundraising for its assistance in the development of this course. The course team would like to acknowledge the contribution of the following authors whose work, ideas and creativity in previous courses have helped shape the thinking behind B625 *Winning Resources and Support*:

Julian Batsleer

Chris Cornforth

Jane Isaacs

Sarabajaya Kumar

Jill Mordaunt

Rob Paton

Alan Thomas

Sue Ward

The Open University
Walton Hall, Milton Keynes
MK7 6AA

First published 2007.

Edited and designed by The Open University.

Typeset in India by Alden Prepress Services, Chennai.

Printed and bound in the United Kingdom by Thanet Press Limited, Margate, Kent.

ISBN 978 0 7492 2400 4

1.1

CONTENTS

INTRODUCTION TO BOOK 6

This book has two main aims:

- to provide you with some practical tools for assessing and determining the strategic options open to your organisation in accessing resources, based on its needs and the opportunities available to it
- to help you to review and synthesise your learning from the course in a way which relates it directly to your professional development.

The first two sessions of this final book of B625 return to the issues of planning and strategy with which we began the course, and which have never been far away from any of its subsequent themes.

The first session deals with ways of looking at an organisation itself (its purpose, requirements and capacities), and with ways of understanding its environment (to discover the opportunities and threats represented by its changing circumstances). This process of analysis provides the foundation for the second session, which considers different forms of strategic responses to the environment. We identify two sets – those which involve competing with other organisations for resources, and those which feature more collaborative approaches. Successful strategy can involve both competitive and collaborative elements, depending on the circumstances.

Strategy is a challenging area for fundraisers and campaigners, and it has important implications. Just as a dogmatically competitive approach can lead to duplication and lack of effectiveness, so an ill-thought-out collaboration can mean that the authentic mission of your organisation gets swamped. Session 2 tries to capture some of the viewpoints in this debate before offering you some strategic templates adapted for the voluntary sector from business models. These are not meant to be bland formulas, but ways of structuring (and sharing) your thinking about your particular situation which can suggest relevant ways forward.

There are only three sessions in this book, compared to the usual four. This is because of the third session's interactive nature – which is likely to involve you in more activity than a standard session. This session brings the theme of planning and strategy to a personal level. It provides an opportunity for you to review your learning from the course and relate it to your current professional situation. You may remember early in the course working through a number of checklists highlighting the different clusters of skills involved in winning resources and support. This final session is an opportunity to gauge your progress, particularly in those areas where your initial diagnosis revealed developmental priorities. The assignments and practical exercises throughout the course books have been aimed at developing your knowledge, understanding and skills in a way that is directly relevant to improving your confidence and performance in fundraising. Reviewing your learning should therefore be a satisfying experience, as well as indicating specific areas for attention during your revision for the examination. Furthermore, given the progressive nature of personal development and fundraising itself, this final review will provide pointers to planning your next steps in continuing professional development.

Session 1

Thinking Strategically: Strategic Analysis

Session 1

CONTENTS

1 THINKING STRATEGICALLY: STRATEGIC ANALYSIS

1.1 INTRODUCTION

Planning enables us to do the right things in the right way for the right reasons at the right time. And planning is linked inextricably to control. If we have an idea of what should be happening (from a plan) we can detect deviations from the plan in time to do something in order to get back on track to achieve our objectives. But how do we know that our objectives are appropriate, and that we are going about achieving them in the right way? We have laid great emphasis in the course so far on the idea of a control loop – but what if the loop means that we are just going round in circles?

This is why we need to think about strategy. Strategy attempts to set a successful direction for an organisation and bring coherence and coordination to the different things it does. In essence strategy ensures that there is a fit between the organisation and its changing environment, as well as between the different parts of the organisation. If an organisation becomes out of tune with the changing needs of its clients, members or donors its chances of success will be greatly diminished. Equally, if the various parts of the organisation are each independently 'doing their own thing' this is a recipe for confusion and inefficiency. Our planning control loop, useful as it is, compares performance against targets. Strategy goes a step further, to ask whether the targets themselves (and our way of achieving them) are still appropriate to what the organisation should be doing.

The amount of time and attention given to strategy varies considerably between organisations. People may feel that they are too busy dealing with day-to-day business or that the future is too uncertain to spend time on developing a strategy. This is often the case in new, smaller organisations, but it is not uncommon elsewhere. In some situations the absence of strategic thinking may seem to make sense, because the environment is only changing very slowly, or is simply too unpredictable. However, the danger is that the organisation will not adapt to changes in its environment or will go off in new and possibly inappropriate directions, and its activities will lack coordination and coherence.

The term 'strategy' has a rather grand ring to it – something for the generals and not the troops. While it is true that the more senior you are within an organisation the more time you are likely to spend on strategy, this view is rather misleading. The complexity of the environment means that those at the top seldom have a monopoly of wisdom. Equally, any strategy is more likely to be implemented successfully if it takes people with it rather than is imposed on them. For these reasons strategies usually evolve through a complex series of discussions and negotiations. If your unit or function has a clear view of its own preferred strategy it will be in a better position to influence the process of formulating the organisation's overall strategy.

An organisation's strategy would normally consider the long-term development of its services and products in response to changing needs, the resources needed to provide them, and the systems and structures needed to put this into effect. So a strategy for winning resources and support is just one part, albeit an important one, of an organisation's overall strategy. It is important to remember that the different components of an organisation's strategy are interdependent. Any fundraising strategy needs to consider other aspects of the organisation's overall strategy as well.

The process of developing a strategy can usefully be divided up into three overlapping phases of *analysis*, *formulation* and *implementation*. These phases form part of a wider loop of control which will include *evaluation* and *reformulation* as appropriate. This session focuses on *strategic analysis* and examines the match between an organisation and its changing environment. The analysis consists of:

- an *organisational assessment* – looking at the capabilities of the organisation to pursue any strategy, focusing in particular on its strengths and weaknesses – and
- an *environmental assessment* – examining changes in the organisation's environment and any new opportunities or threats that are likely to emerge from this.

Analysing an organisation's Strengths and Weaknesses, Opportunities and Threats is often called SWOT analysis. An extension of this approach is presented here.

Aims and learning outcomes

This session has three aims:

- to describe the different aspects of carrying out a strategic analysis in relation to winning resources and support
- to introduce the idea of an organisational assessment and to present a framework for carrying one out
- to introduce the idea of environmental analysis and consider some concepts that are useful for analysing external influences that may affect an organisation's ability to win resources and support.

After studying this session you should be able to:

- specify the factors that need to be considered when carrying out an organisational assessment
- make a preliminary assessment of your organisation's main strengths and weaknesses with respect to winning resources and support

- use the STEP model to explore the possible impact of wider environmental changes on your organisation and its capacity to win resources and support
- identify your organisation's operating environment and make a preliminary assessment of what new opportunities and threats it is likely to face with respect to winning resources and support
- summarise the results of an organisational and environmental assessment on a SWOT diagram.

1.2 ORGANISATIONAL ASSESSMENT: DETERMINING STRENGTHS AND WEAKNESSES

The strategy that your organisation develops for winning resources and support must take account of the organisation as a whole – what it does, what it hopes to achieve in the future, the resources it has available, its strengths and weaknesses. These characteristics will affect planning at strategic, business and operational levels – but have a particular relevance to fundraising as they determine both the need and the ability of the organisation to access resources. As a result any resource-winning strategy needs to be based on an organisational assessment. Such an assessment can be divided into five main areas:

1. overall mission and strategy (are they appropriate?)
2. resource requirements (are they realistic?)
3. policies and norms (are they fit for purpose?)
4. performance (how well is the organisation doing?)
5. capacities (i.e. resources, systems and structures – what is the organisation capable of as it stands?)

We will now look at these five aspects of organisational assessment in more detail.

1.2.1 The organisation's overall mission and strategy

Winning resources and support is a means to an end, rather than an end in itself. Any strategy for winning resources must start from the wider needs it is seeking to meet. It is only by understanding these that you will be able to appreciate your organisation's long-term requirements for resources and support. And without such an appreciation, you stand little chance of making a convincing case to donors and supporters. A careful and considered mission statement is likely to be an important asset in this process. Stephen Bubb, chief executive of the Association of Chief Executives of Voluntary Organisations (ACEVO) highlights the importance of an effective mission statement in Box 1.1.

BOX 1.1

THE MISSION STATEMENT

The point of a mission statement is to set out the focus and direction for the organisation. The idea is to encapsulate within a neat sentence or paragraph your main objective. That statement is then used to inform customers, clients and stakeholders about you.

If you have not got a mission statement, the process of drawing one up can often be useful in itself. It is an excellent focus for a staff discussion, at an away day for example. It would be good to involve your trustees and other stakeholders.

We often get too tied down in day-to-day operational matters and sometimes lose sight of our strategic direction. So a discussion about the overall focus can be used to generate ideas about where the organisation is going, how it is doing and what needs to change.

It is certainly true that if an organisation loses sight of its objectives, then it can atrophy or die. Being clear of your purpose is vital for success.

(Source: Bubb, 2002)

Of course, this is not just a one-way process. Developing a strategy for winning resources and support should contribute to the organisation's overall mission and strategy. In particular, it should tell you how feasible it is to generate the resources and support needed to meet other long-term goals. If it looks as though these resources cannot be generated then other long-term goals may have to be revised. The links between a strategy for winning resources and support and the organisation's overall mission and strategy are shown in Figure 1.1.

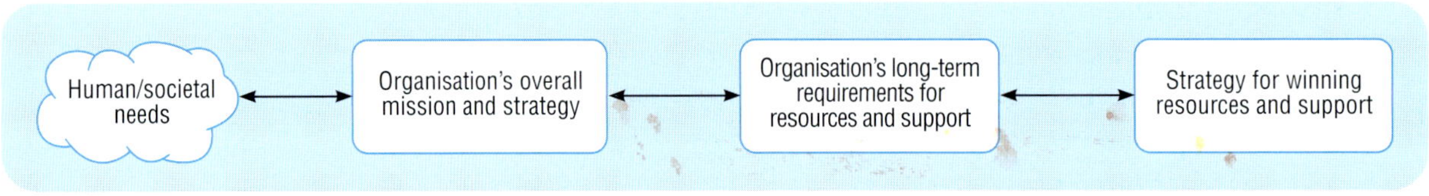

Figure 1.1 The links between an organisation's overall strategy and its strategy for winning resources and support

Your organisation's mission and goals may also place constraints upon how resources and support are raised. Van der Gaag (2007) argues that certain sorts of emotive images in fundraising publicity can be counterproductive to the mission and long-term goals of development organisations, for example, and any organisation's ethical policy will have implications for its fundraising and campaigning work.

Not all organisations have a clearly articulated mission and long-term goals, or these may be surrounded by disagreement and uncertainty. In such a situation it will be more difficult to work out what are appropriate long-term goals for winning resources and support. As a result you may have to spend time trying to get your organisation to clarify its goals and purposes, or operate in a more short-term and uncertain environment.

ACTIVITY 1.1

(a) Thinking about your organisation, or another that you know well, does it have a mission statement and agreed long-term goals?

(b) If yes, what do you think are the main implications for winning resources and support over the next two to five years?

(c) If no, what do you think can be done to help clarify the organisation's mission and long-term goals? What do you think a mission statement for the organisation should emphasise?

Of course, your answer to this question will depend on the organisation in question. Even what an organisation calls a mission statement will vary from one situation to another. Some prefer the term 'vision statement', others will see it as the basis of the case statement – as described in Book 2.

A popular template for a concise mission statement is to say what you do, how you do it and who you do it for. The need to be clear about the answers to these questions has become more pressing in the UK for charities since the publication in 2000 of the Statement of Recommended Practice (SORP) by the Charity Commission, setting out an accounting and reporting framework to increase transparency in annual reports. Amongst other requirements it demands that charities provide an account of their performance against their objectives.

1.2.2 The organisation's resource requirements

The organisation's overall strategy should indicate what the organisation's long-term requirements for resources are. However, it is necessary not just to understand the total amount of money required, but also how it is to be used, as this often has an important influence on what sources of funds and methods of fundraising are appropriate. For example, many trusts and foundations prefer to support innovative programmes rather than sustain existing core operations; legacy income is often too unpredictable to support core operating costs.

It is important, then, to categorise your organisation's financial needs into different types. One useful way of doing this is to distinguish between:

- *capital expenses* (e.g. buildings, equipment)
- *core operating costs* (the costs of running the organisation's core operations and associated administrative and support services), and
- one-off *project costs* (e.g. a short-term pilot project).

The precise categorisation appropriate to your organisation will depend on its circumstances. However, it is vital to distinguish between core operating costs, which are recurrent, and other one-off forms of expenditure.

When devising a fundraising strategy, it is particularly important to consider how your core operating costs are going to be met. As these costs are long term you should be looking for long-term income to meet them. So it is vital to look at your organisation's major funders and how you can develop a long-term relationship with them.

It is true, however, that many donors and funders prefer to give money for specific projects or other short-term forms of expenditure. We have discussed elsewhere in the course the predicament this creates for fundraisers. While one can understand the desire of funders to encourage innovative projects rather than pay for what has already been established (particularly given the blurring of boundaries between statutory and voluntary sector provision), the result of many funding policies is that continuing services have to be regularly rebranded as a series of fixed-life projects in order to attract grants. Certainly, realistic overhead costs need to be built into applications for project funding as a means of helping to cover the core costs of the organisation without which the projects would be unworkable.

ACTIVITY 1.2

1 Thinking of your organisation, or another which you know well, what sources of funds and methods of fundraising are used to meet its core operating costs? (Just list the main types rather than go into detail.)

2 How secure do you think these sources of funds are in the long term?

3 What do you think might be done to safeguard long-term income?

As we have discussed, providing for core operating costs is one of the biggest challenges facing fundraisers in any organisation. While clearly charities have a duty to be as efficient as possible in order to concentrate their resources on the needs they exist to satisfy, it sometimes seems that there is an expectation they should do without central administration. Fundraising sources that can help to meet core costs include regular, committed giving schemes (such as payroll giving), income from trading, and subscriptions. Contracts are a way of resourcing longer-term core costs, but they often involve taking on commitments and infrastructure which remain the voluntary organisation's responsibility if and when the contract ends. No source of funding is 100 per cent secure in the long term, so it is important to diversify the portfolio of fundraising activities appropriate to your organisation's capacities, rather than rely on just a narrow range. We will return to this idea of portfolio management in the next session.

1.2.3 Policies and norms

In fundraising and campaigning, as with many other activities, our actions are limited by various constraints. Important among these are the policies and norms that prevail within an organisation.

Many voluntary and not-for-profit organisations have found it necessary to develop policies and guidelines that define what sorts of practices are acceptable when trying to win resources and support. Here is a reminder of some reasons why such policies and guidelines can be useful:

- *To maintain integrity* – They can help the organisation avoid accepting resources or support from sources whose activities might conflict with the aims of the organisation. For example, many charities may have a policy of not accepting gifts from tobacco companies, and campaigning organisations may not accept sponsorship from commercial organisations if they feel that might jeopardise their independence. Codes of practice, such as those established by the UK's Institute of Fundraising, are particularly useful in this regard.
- *To ensure consistency* – If all staff are aware of your organisation's policies and guidelines on what sorts of gifts and support are acceptable and how they should be handled, it will help to ensure that supporters and donors are treated in a consistent and equitable manner. For example, a university will usually have guidelines about the appropriate levels of funding required to establish a lectureship or professorial chair.
- *To provide ready authoritative answers* – A policy can provide useful guidance to staff and volunteers faced with unfamiliar circumstances. It can also provide a courteous way of refusing certain gifts without alienating potential donors. For example, a museum may want to have a policy on refusing works of art that do not fit the needs of its particular collection.
- *To help coordinate activities* – A policy can spell out who should undertake which activities, for example, who should speak to the press, or who can approach certain donors.

Of course, many organisations do not have formal policies with regard to winning resources and support. However, it is likely that over time some informal agreements or norms will have developed about what is acceptable practice and what is not. The trouble with informal rules is that they are not very visible. You may only become aware of the rules when you break them and your activities or proposals are criticised. Sometimes, though, informality can be an advantage – it may allow incremental changes in 'policy' without the agony of having to negotiate an explicit change in direction.

ACTIVITY 1.3

(a) Thinking of your organisation, or another with which you are familiar, does it have any formal policies with regard to winning resources and support? If so, can you give an example of how this has affected fundraising or campaigning work in the recent past?

(b) Are you aware of any informal norms or rules about what it is acceptable or unacceptable to do in your chosen organisation with regard to winning resources and support? If so, what are they and how do they constrain such activity?

Organisations vary considerably in the importance they attach to developing formal policies. However, it is true to say that the larger the organisation the more likely it is to have formal policies. The Open University, for example, has a set of explicit guidelines on the use of images in its fundraising and promotional work in order to preserve its brand identity and to ensure that its commitment to equal opportunities and diversity is properly expressed.

By their very nature you only really get to know about informal norms and rules by observing custom and practice in an organisation. If you are new to your organisation, or are unsure about what practices are acceptable, you may want to talk this issue over with an experienced colleague or manager.

1.2.4 Analysing performance

To determine the best way to win resources or support for your organisation, or the cause that it serves, it is important to have an understanding of how it performs. Obviously, it is important to know about the organisation's history of fundraising, campaigning and promotional work, to know what has worked well in the past and what lessons can be learned. But it is also important to know about other aspects of the organisation's performance that may be of interest to potential supporters and donors.

The relative strengths and weaknesses of what your organisation does can be assessed by answering the following questions:

- What are the organisation's aims and objectives?
- How well does your organisation serve the needs of its clients or promote the cause that it serves? Clearly, if you can argue that your organisation is effective and compares well with other similar organisations, you will be able to present strong reasons why your organisation deserves support. It is also important to ask what is distinctive or innovative about your organisation. If it is pioneering or doing things that others are unable to do there may again be good arguments for giving it support.
- How efficiently does your organisation use its resources? Is the organisation well managed? Is it financially sound? No donor or supporter is going to want to give money or support to an organisation that is inefficient or is likely to fail. If your

organisation is large or well established you may not have difficulty in demonstrating its credibility. New or smaller organisations may find that they have to spend much more effort in this area. For example, it is usual for major donors to want to see some kind of business plan for the organisation or a particular project so that they can assess the viability of particular initiatives and have some reassurance that their money will be well spent.

- How successful have past strategies for winning resources and support been? What aspects worked well, what aspects worked less well, and why? If you know what your strengths are you can build on them. Equally, if you know your weaknesses you can either take steps to overcome them or avoid similar initiatives in future.
- What mix of sources of resources and support does your organisation draw upon? As we have argued earlier, a potential danger for any organisation is to be dependent on just a few sources of income, because if anything happens to threaten support from these sources it will have a major impact on the organisation, perhaps endangering its very existence. Reducing dependence and trying to secure a broad mix of different forms of support and funding is an important strategic consideration for any organisation.

ACTIVITY 1.4

Give an example of some evidence you could use to help convince a potential donor or supporter that an organisation is:

(a) effective in achieving its main goals

(b) efficient and well managed.

When considering effectiveness, it is easier to measure outputs than outcomes. For example, a development charity like Save the Children Fund can count the number of wells it has helped dig in a year (an output), but the impact this makes on improving children's life chances (an outcome) is more difficult to quantify. Effectiveness, therefore, may have to rely on proxy measures.

Efficiency is another thorny topic. Emphasising simple measures of efficiency, such as percentage of donation value applied directly to the cause, or the ratio of expenditure to income, runs the risk of feeding prejudices against funding perfectly legitimate core costs, or ignoring the variable circumstances under which money is raised. As with any of the four Es of effectiveness, efficiency, economy and ethics, an exclusive concentration on one measure can be misleading.

1.2.5 Analysing organisational capacities

As you saw in the last section, any plan needs to be based on a realistic assessment of the organisation's capacity to carry it out. Strategy is no exception. For example, it would be foolish to embark on a strategy which centred on direct mail if the organisation did not have the financial resources to sustain it during the initial period before the initial investment began to pay back. Similarly, it is no good developing a strategy which relies on a range of local events if you do not have a committed base of volunteers and the organisational capacity to support them.

When assessing your unit or organisation's capacities it is important to consider a number of different aspects and questions. These are discussed below.

Organisational image

What images, positive and negative, does the public hold of your organisation or the cause that it serves? Answers to questions like these will have an important bearing on the feasibility of various strategies, and explain why branding is so important for charities and other fundraising organisations. For example, it will be difficult to embark on various forms of public fundraising, such as collections, if there is very little public awareness of your organisation and the cause that it serves. Conversely, if your organisation has a positive image and high public awareness, many more options will be available. The International Federation of Red Cross and Red Crescent Societies have such a salient image that when there is a disaster somewhere in the world people donate spontaneously to them, even before their deliberate fundraising work starts.

Human resources

What human resources are available – trustees, patrons, staff, volunteers and other supporters? How much time do they have available and when? What expertise can they contribute? What support do they require?

Financial resources

How much money is available for capital and running costs to implement the strategy? Over what period is it available? What sort of 'return' on investment is the organisation looking for? What are the cash flow implications of your proposals?

Systems and technology

What systems and technology exist within the organisation to support any strategy for winning resources and support? For example, does the organisation have some kind of database of donors and supporters, and how up to date is this? Does the organisation have systems for dealing with and processing large numbers of members, donors and supporters?

Structures

Any strategic review should also be looking at how the organisation is structured and how to get the best out of its different parts. For example, if your organisation has regional or local branches you will need to consider which activities are best carried out centrally and which locally.

ACTIVITY 1.5

Again, thinking of your own organisation or one with which you are familiar, consider what capacities it has available for winning resources or support. List below what you think are its main strengths and weaknesses in this respect.

Strengths:

Weaknesses:

Of course, the idea of strengths and weaknesses will be relative to the purposes of the organisation. Box 1.2 describes an organisation called Karuna Trust. It gives an idea of some of Karuna Trust's strengths and weaknesses. How does it compare with those of the unit or organisation you chose for Activity 1.5?

BOX 1.2

AN ORGANISATIONAL ASSESSMENT AT KARUNA TRUST

The Karuna Trust started life as Aid for India in 1980. Founded and administered by Western Buddhists, it promotes dignity, self-confidence and the breaking down of caste and religious barriers. Its projects are open to everyone in need, regardless of background. It now works with some of the poorest communities in India, creating education, health and cultural projects to promote dignity and self-reliance. It employs a handful of staff in the UK and its income and expenditure are in the order of £750,000 per year.

The Trust was formed by a group of British Buddhists from the Western Order of Buddhists who had been moved by the suffering of the 'untouchables' in Pune, India. They had come to Pune to teach aspects of Buddhism to those who had been converted to Buddhism by the Indian social reformer Dr Ambedkar in 1956. This conversion was a deliberate way of giving them a new status to help them break out of the rigid caste system, and it had been achieved by a dramatic process of mass conversions.

Fundraising for Aid for India was conducted in the UK and after a time began to concentrate on door-to-door fundraising, which simulated, in a well-thought-out and carefully managed programme, the traditional method of seeking alms practised by Buddhists in the East. This became a strong source of income based on committed tax-efficient giving and Karuna's income grew steadily.

The key request of the local population (in the slums of Dapodi outside Pune) concerned child health and this was the focus of early investigations. It was found that there were high levels of malnutrition, low rates of vaccination and a lot of night blindness due to vitamin A deficiency, and these problems were often made worse by poor infant feeding practices. The early work of Karuna therefore concentrated on health delivery through teams of trained local health workers.

As time passed it became clear that children were not accessing mainstream educational facilities because of their status. Karuna answered this problem by establishing kindergartens which issued educational certificates. These were accepted by government schools in lieu of birth certificates, and this concept then became widespread in the area.

Soon after, Karuna began to establish hostels for high school students to enable them to access government-provided education. Poor rural children as well as those from the slums took advantage of these hostels, which also provided cultural activities. By 2000 Karuna contributed to 18 hostels and supported projects in eight of the Indian states.

There were, almost inevitably, problems due to the rapid growth of the organisation. For example, there were tensions between those responsible for the running of the hostel programmes and the local communities they served. In the 1990s there was only one organisation in India responsible for all of the programmes.

The problems of growth were tackled by instituting a period of slowing down to allow for structural change, which then opened the way to fund a variety of partners in India. This allowed for new projects to be developed including community saving schemes, cooperative banks and cultural programmes, increasing the range and variety of projects. Help was also extended to poor Tibetan refugee families.

Diversification of income was needed and grants were sought from the Department for International Development, the European Union and other institutional funders. The lack of variety in income sources remained, however, a weakness: especially as the more recent converts to Buddhism were increasingly reluctant to fundraise door to door.

ACTIVITY 1.6

Having read the account of the Karuna Trust in Box 1.2, how would you analyse the organisation according to the headings for organisational assessment given earlier in Section 1.2?

Mission and strategy:

Resource requirements:

Policies and norms:

Performance:

Capacities (organisational image, human resources, financial resources, systems and technology, structures):

Here are some points you might have picked up – and you may have more of your own.

Mission and strategy: overcoming disadvantage amongst low-caste groups in society through projects in education, health and culture, to promote dignity and self-reliance.

Resource requirements: currently £750,000 per year – but a need to diversify income sources is evident as new projects are initiated and existing ones developed.

Policies and norms: the organisation is rooted very clearly in Buddhist traditions. This affects its mission as well as its traditional approach to gathering alms door to door.

Performance: effective, but the rapid growth in activities described here threatened to make the organisation a victim of its own success. So a need to slow down is evident. The history of the organisation's performance demonstrates a move away from centrally-run projects to working in cooperation with local partners.

Capacities: The image of the organisation is an attractive one – 'Karuna' means 'love' in the Buddhist tradition. Human resources now centre on partnerships with local organisations and workers, with a small core team based in the UK. Financial resources are in the region of £750,000 per year – but there is an acknowledged need to diversify the funding base. Systems and technology appear to be appropriate to the needs met, but in need of development in order to address the fundraising problem. Structures seem effective in delivering relevant services.

1.3 ENVIRONMENTAL ANALYSIS: DETERMINING OPPORTUNITIES AND THREATS

Modern society is often characterised by rapid change – economic, technical and social changes seem to occur more and more rapidly. These changes may bring about both new opportunities and threats to organisations. The challenge for any organisation is to be sufficiently aware of the changes so that it can take advantage of new opportunities and deal with any threats. The danger for less-aware organisations is that they may stagnate, or indeed that their survival may be threatened.

This section will look at some of the things that can be done to keep abreast of changes in the environment that might affect what you do. We will distinguish between different aspects of an organisation's environment, as shown in Figure 1.2.

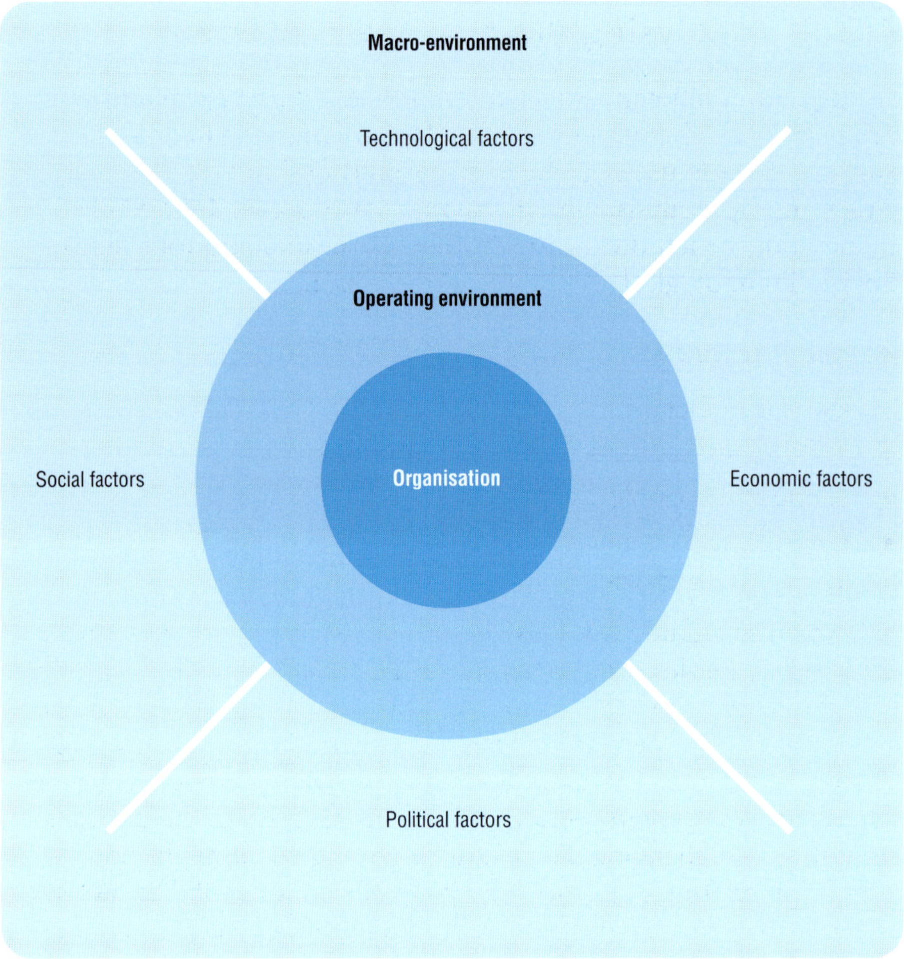

Figure 1.2 A model of an organisation's environment

First, there is what we can term the organisation's *operating environment*. This consists of:

- those with whom your organisation interacts while doing work (other agencies, clients, funders, suppliers, etc.)
- actual and potential competitors and collaborators
- public institutions that watch or regulate what organisations like your own do (for example, the Charity Commission in England and Wales). Brewster (2007, p. 203) refers to 'institutional environment' to mean the players in a particular field of operation and their relative power and influence. The term 'institutional environment' can also be used to refer to the kind of arrangements which underpin funding arrangements between such organisations (in the sense of legal 'institutions' such as contracts). For example, a move from grant-aid to contracting for services has been a change in the institutional environment affecting the relationship between local government and voluntary organisations in the UK from the late twentieth century onwards. Institutional environment is thus an important part of the operating environment of fundraising in either of its senses.

Second, there is the wider *macro-environment*. This consists of the broader societal forces, such as economic or demographic changes, that confront the organisation either directly or through influencing its operating environment.

1.3.1 Analysing the macro-environment

Clearly many different environmental factors have the potential to affect an organisation and what it does to win resources and support. So it is useful to have some kind of framework to structure any analysis. One in common use is called the STEP framework, which divides environmental factors into four kinds: Social, Technological, Economic and Political.

Social factors

Social factors include:

- changes in people's values and attitudes
- changes in people's lifestyles
- demographic changes (e.g. changes in the size, distribution and age of the population).

The public's attitude towards a cause is clearly an important factor influencing the level of giving and support for the cause. It is clear too that some causes are easier to gain public sympathy for than others. However, perceptions vary between different groups and change over time. Therefore to maximise opportunities for gaining support it is important periodically to monitor social attitudes and how they are changing. For example (strange as it might now seem), pioneering anti-smoking groups faced a credibility problem when canvassing for support back in the 1970s, but now attitudes are very different. Similarly, many environmental pressure groups were seen as radical idealists when they originally campaigned for green policies, but now are regarded as part of the mainstream.

Demographic trends such as changes in the age profile, family size, work patterns and income levels of the population are also important. For example, it may be appropriate to target fundraising on groups with high levels of disposable income. Demographic changes may mean that the importance of particular causes changes. For example, the ageing of the population in Western Europe means that there is likely to be growing public concern about the levels of support for the elderly. Voluntary and not-for-profit organisations have also been concerned for some time that demographic changes will affect the availability of volunteers. Many organisations are heavily dependent on women volunteers, but changing social attitudes towards women and work, and the decline in the number of school leavers, has meant that more women are taking up paid employment. The threat to voluntary organisations is that there is increasing competition for their traditional pool of voluntary labour.

In examining the social environment of an organisation, the following questions come into play:

- What is the dominant attitude towards the cause?
- Do different groups hold different attitudes towards the cause?
- Are these attitudes changing and is there any trend?
- How are demographic changes likely to affect the organisation's activities?

ACTIVITY 1.7

(a) Thinking of your own organisation, or another which you know well, what do you think have been the most important social factors that have affected its ability to win resources and support in recent years?

(b) What social factors do you think are likely to affect its ability to win resources and support in the next five years?

You may be interested to compare your responses with the suggestions in Box 1.3, inspired by a report from a consultancy which specialises in considering the future of the voluntary sector. The aim of this Activity and those that follow it in this section based on STEP factors is not that you should be able to predict change accurately, but be aware of the sorts of changes you need to keep alert for.

BOX 1.3

SOCIAL CHANGE AND THE FUTURE OF FUNDRAISING

Evans and Saxton (2003) argue that fundraisers need to pay more attention than ever to 'life course'. Social change will require increased sensitivity to what potential donors and volunteers want at different stages in their lives. The main factors will be an ageing population, changing family structures (as marital ties become more fluid), and an increasingly well-educated (and indebted) younger generation. The consequences of such changes all point the same way – people of all ages will make greater demands on charities, as clients, donors and/or volunteers.

Older people will live longer, which may mean that assets such as property and investments, key resources for charities targeting legacies, are consumed in care-home fees rather than left in wills. But these same older people will remain healthier for longer in their retirement, creating new resources of time and skills for charities keen to recruit volunteers. It's likely that older people, and their families, will have a much more guarded attitude to wealth – and thus a less spontaneous approach to giving.

Changing family structures will alter the kind of relationships on which, for example, the 'contribution multiplier' depends. Fundraising in schools and communities, or at particular times of the year, cannot afford to take traditional family ties for granted. One consequence could be charities continuing to take ever more direct responsibility for running events on a national rather than local basis.

As for the educated but indebted younger generation, it may be that some, faced with student debts and rising house prices, will take a 'holiday' from any kind of charitable giving altogether. This will pose a considerable challenge to fundraisers to ensure they are not permanently lost as donors.

Evans and Saxton's prediction is that fundraising success will come from understanding changing wants and needs over time, and adapting fundraising products to match them. So, for example, we can expect to see such things as charity catalogues, overseas challenge events and membership schemes being much more closely targeted to particular demographic groups than has been the case previously. We may even be witnessing the start of the demise of the kind of 'mass fundraising' which has been an important element in the resource base of many a household name in charity (and lent such organisations a great deal of their legitimacy).

(Source: adapted from Evans and Saxton, 2003).

Technological factors

No organisation can afford to ignore technological change if it wishes to remain efficient and effective. Changing technology has had an impact on fundraising, public relations and campaigning, as on other aspects of organisational life. The development of sophisticated databases handling a variety of information about people has enabled organisations of all sizes to target potential new donors and supporters more easily. The rapid growth in the use of the internet and email has led to new forms of campaigning and fundraising. Mobile telephony and allied technologies (which are constantly converging into new configurations) have provided a completely new way of contacting potential donors in age groups which have proved difficult to reach using more traditional methods.

When scrutinising the technological environment of an organisation, relevant questions are:

- What technology does it use at present for winning resources and support, and how is it developing?
- Are other organisations, in this country or abroad, making use of other newer technologies?
- Are there other new technologies that could usefully be exploited?

ACTIVITY 1.8

(a) Thinking of your own organisation, or another which you know well, what do you think have been the most important technological factors that have affected its ability to win resources and support in recent years?

(b) What technological factors do you think are likely to affect winning resources and support in the organisation in the next five years?

Economic factors

Economic trends are relevant to how willing or likely people are to give. Trends in personal wealth, employment, consumption, and disposable income have an effect on all categories of givers – whether they be organisations, trusts or individuals. In the case of individuals, the 'feel-good factor', prized by political pollsters as a mark of success in economic policy, is likely to dispose individuals towards giving. By contrast, periods of economic uncertainty mean that individuals rein back their expenditure – on charity as well as other areas of discretionary spending.

When analysing the economic environment of an organisation the sorts of questions to ask are:

- What is the economic outlook in the immediate future?
- What are the economy's longer-term prospects?
- In what different ways will these economic changes affect the organisation's usual sources of funds and demand for services?

ACTIVITY 1.9

(a) Thinking of your own organisation, or another which you know well, what do you think have been the most important economic factors that have affected its ability to win resources and support in recent years?

(b) What economic factors do you think are likely to affect its ability to win resources in the next five years?

Political factors

Political factors, particularly the government and the policies it pursues, are a significant influence on voluntary and not-for-profit organisations and the public sector. In the UK and many other parts of Europe, the twenty-first century has seen governments keen to incorporate voluntary and community organisations ever more closely in their plans to deliver public services. This is not only on the grounds of cost effectiveness, but also because of a conviction that such organisations can work in contexts in which more formal organisations might encounter resistance. Such partnerships can be uneven, however. Government influence on voluntary and not-for-profit organisations is exerted in a variety of ways, for example:

- through the direct funding of many organisations by both central and local government, as well as regional bodies such as the European Union
- through setting the regulatory and legislative framework within which they must operate (e.g. data protection and human rights legislation)
- through tax concessions on voluntary donations to charities
- through establishing the general level and pattern of provision of public services and the instruments by which they are funded (which involves the 'institutional environment' of legal arrangements governing funding relationships)
- through setting the agenda in areas such as child care, alcohol and drugs services, and medical care.

When examining the political environment the sorts of questions that a fundraiser will want to ask are:

- How are changes in the different tiers of government, such as the growing importance of international and regional legislation, likely to affect the organisation's activities?
- Are there any proposals for new legislation that will affect its service delivery, campaigning or fundraising?
- What changes are happening in government programmes, funding or tax concessions that are likely to affect such activities?
- What capacity does the organisation have to influence political decisions that affect it, and can this capacity be developed?

ACTIVITY 1.10

(a) Thinking of your own organisation, or another which you know well, what do you think have been the most important political factors that have affected its ability to win resources and support in recent years?

(b) What political factors do you think are likely to affect your chosen organisation's ability to win resources and support in the next five years?

1.3.2 Analysing the operating environment

This section will look in more detail at the operating environment. The operating environment can be considered in terms of:

- *The resource domain* – This consists of the various sources of funds and resources that the organisation may draw upon.
- *The decision domain* – This consists of the various organisations, groups and individuals that the organisation may try to influence to support its cause.
- *The service domain* – This consists of the various organisations, groups and individuals that the organisation may serve.
- *The competition* – This consists of the *competitors* the organisation faces in each of these domains.

The resource domain

There are five main sources of resources – statutory bodies, companies, trusts and foundations, associations, and individuals – and a variety of different forms in which this support may be given (related to the 'institutional environment' mentioned in the previous section). These are summarised in Table 1.1. The purpose of analysing how the resource domain is changing is to try to identify whether there are new opportunities for gaining resources or any threats to existing resources.

Table 1.1 Sources of resources and the forms in which they are given

Sources	Forms of support
Statutory bodies (e.g. European Commission, central government departments, local authorities, health authorities)	Matching funds Grants Service agreements Contracts
Companies	Contracts Donations – gifts, committed giving, etc. Employee fundraising and volunteering Gifts in kind Licensing Promotions Secondments Sponsorships
Trusts and foundations	Grants – capital/revenue, regular/ phased/occasional/one-off Matching funds, etc.
Associations (e.g. churches, schools, trades unions, rotary clubs)	Donations Gifts in kind Special campaigns/events Raising awareness
Individuals	Donations – gifts, tax-effective giving, legacies, etc. Gifts in kind Membership Response to trading, events, etc. Voluntary help

In looking at the resource domain for a particular organisation the important questions are:

- What existing sources of funding and other support does the organisation rely on, and what forms do they take?
- How are these sources likely to be affected by changes in STEP factors?
- What sources do similar (competing) organisations rely upon? (This may give a fundraiser some ideas about new sources of funds that their organisation could tap.)
- Are there any new sources of funding or other emerging forms of support that the organisation could exploit?

The decision domain

The decision domain will be of particular interest to those whose job involves campaigning or promotional work. It consists of the various individuals, groups and other organisations an organisation may try to influence to support its cause, for example members, the public, politicians, government, and the media.

In assessing the decision domain the important questions are:

- What groups or organisations does the organisation rely on to support its cause?
- Who are the key people in these groups or organisations?
- How are these different sources of support being affected by changes in STEP factors? (Are public attitudes changing in such a way as to enhance or decrease support for a particular cause? How will political changes, such as a change of government, or the replacement of a key decision-maker, affect support?)
- What sources of support do similar (competing) organisations rely on?

The service domain

The service domain may not be the main focus of interest for a fundraiser or campaigner. Yet it is important that anyone involved in winning resources and support has a good knowledge of what their organisation does and the needs it is trying to meet. Potential donors and supporters will want to know why they should support a particular organisation or cause, and they need to be given a convincing answer. This means close liaison for fundraisers and campaigners with other parts of their organisations. In addition, changing needs and patterns of service provision may provide new opportunities for winning new donors and supporters.

The competition

The nature and intensity of competition from other organisations will also impact on strategy. There is a good deal of evidence to suggest that the level of competition for resources and support is continuing to grow as the number of activities covered by the voluntary sector increases. Perhaps just as important has been the growing number of organisations in the public sector, such as hospitals, schools, universities and colleges that are also competing for resources. The idea of good causes being in competition with one another, so that there are winners and losers, is not very palatable to many people working in the voluntary sector. This point is eloquently expressed in Box 1.4.

BOX 1.4

UNCOMFORTABLE COMPETITION

When I hear the phrase 'cut-throat competition', I either think of supermarkets fighting to offer baked beans at the lowest possible prices, or clashes between corporate giants desperate to put each other out of business. In short, when that phrase arises, the voluntary sector does not readily come to mind.

However, it has long been recognised that we are all fighting for a finite amount of money and support. Many once-reliable income generators, such as local branches, street collections and legacies are changing or drying up. Greater competition, people living longer and an increasing need for older people to pay for their own care have all eaten into traditional sources of funds and, in turn, have led to even greater competition.

Clearly, the voluntary sector has to be market-driven and competition is an integral part of that. At the heart of voluntary organisations is the aim of working for the common good. In the rush for people's hearts, minds and wallets, we must avoid undermining those with whom we compete.

To those used to the world of hostile corporate takeovers, that may seem a naive hope, but the sector's adoption of commercial business practices is appropriate only if it helps us all to achieve our aims of social empowerment, advocacy and innovation in service provision.

We need to work alongside the corporate and statutory sectors as equal partners, with a clear idea of our own identity and what we want to achieve.

If we allow our business methods and practices to slide into an uncritical mirror image of the other sectors, there is a danger that we will lose sight of what sets us apart.

The voluntary sector places people above all else. In increasing our efficiency and effectiveness, we must treat stakeholders and competitors alike with the respect that our sector is associated with.

Voluntary organisations should work together to develop both an understanding of our sector and an understanding of what a fairer world entails and how it might be achieved. However, while it is important, the concept of fairness is not the only reason to show respect. It is one of our sector's unique selling points and, as such, could be commercial gold dust.

(Source: Peacock, 2002)

Quite apart from competition from other charities and good causes for scarce resources, voluntary and community organisations also face indirect competition from leisure, entertainment, sports, and even education. All are the basis of substantial industries whose survival depends on gaining a share of people's minds, hearts and wallets. Growing competition has increased pressures towards the professionalisation of activities such as fundraising and charity retailing. Fundraising activities may also require greater levels of investment to realise the same levels of return as they have in the past.

Comparing itself to others (external benchmarking as discussed in Book 5) may provide insights into how an organisation might improve its competitive position. For example, a major national charity observed that income from legacies was one of the fastest growing areas of charity funds, yet it raised substantially less from this source than many other leading national charities did. As a result it took a strategic decision to improve and increase investment in this particular aspect of its fundraising, and has managed to increase the funds it raises significantly.

The exact nature of the comparisons with others that an organisation will want to make will depend on what it is interested in. However, generally useful questions include:

- How well does the organisation perform compared with similar organisations? (For example, how well does it serve the needs of its clients?)
- What, if anything, is distinctive or different about what the organisation does?
- How do its strategies and methods for winning resources and support compare with other similar organisations? (For example, methods used, volunteer help, response rates, returns on investment?)
- How do its efforts to promote its cause compare with those of other organisations? (For example, the quality of annual reports, advertisements or other promotional literature?)
- Are there areas of activity that are becoming overcrowded and that it should consider abandoning?
- Are there areas where it might do better to collaborate with other organisations rather than compete?

ACTIVITY 1.11

(a) Thinking of your own organisation, or another which you know well, write down who you think are its main competitors for resources and/or support.

(b) What, if any, influence do you think changing patterns of competition will have on this in the next year or two?

(c) Note any areas where you feel the organisation could learn from its competitors.

Your answers to these questions will depend on the particular circumstances or your chosen organisation. However, general trends might include the way that increased competition is leading to greater professionalism and training in all aspects of winning resources and support. Many organisations are also placing a greater emphasis on developing long-term relationships with donors and supporters.

Box 1.5 contains information from an example of an environmental analysis carried out at Karuna Trust.

BOX 1.5

ENVIRONMENTAL ANALYSIS AT KARUNA TRUST

Karuna Trust is fundraising in a very competitive market. The UK has a wide variety of Buddhist organisations and many nationally known development organisations. There is also a perceived fall-off in revenue from alternative funding sources such as direct mail and strong competition from 'face-to-face' fundraising in High Streets. Other organisations are also moving into door-to-door fundraising. The cost of entry to new fundraising operations like direct marketing is high with a profit, typically, only being made after two years of investment.

It is now thought to be much harder to raise funds for social projects in India than in the 1980s. This may be due to generational changes, as those who came of age in the 1960s (and supported Karuna in its early years) were very aware of India and responsive to its needs. There are also many people from low-caste backgrounds who are successful and respected professionals and academics making the cause less emotionally attractive than it has been.

India itself has grown more prosperous and presents a less needy picture to funders, though much of its poverty remains as deep-rooted as before. The economic success that India has had in areas like IT and call centres has to a large extent obscured the very sharp division of wealth between those able to access the rapidly developing modern economy and those excluded from it. Both India and Taiwan (which has an affluent Buddhist community) are possible places in which to develop future income-generating activities. Indeed, wealthy Buddhist organisations in Taiwan have already been tapped for certain projects.

Accountability becomes increasingly difficult over distance and across so many projects and provinces. Yet accountability and credibility are increasingly important for major donors. At one time in Karuna, it could be said of money 'if they needed it we sent it'. This is no longer the case without a rigorous assessment of needs and a clear programme for the efficient and effective use of the funds requested. Skills transfer has, however, sometimes proved difficult as professions like accountancy were not undertaken by or for untouchables.

All partners are held to be part of the same Sanga or Buddhist family and are therefore much closer than traditional development charities might be to the organisations they fund. This gives huge benefits in the ability to develop common understanding, trust and agreed goals but may also have the weakness that it is psychologically harder to set up strong checks and balances with individual operational units within the Sanga.

Politically, India has opened up considerably and it is much easier to communicate, travel and move funds than when Karuna started. Advances in technology have assisted this process, yet there can still be problems. Communication by email, for example, requires a working power source and may not be regarded with the same importance as communication by phone or in person. Distance still acts as a considerable barrier to achievements on the ground.

Activity 1.12 contains a partly completed SWOT diagram for Karuna Trust which has featured as a case study throughout this session. Look at the diagram and then have a go at Activity 1.12 as a way of consolidating your understanding from this session.

ACTIVITY 1.12

Look back at the organisational assessment and environmental analysis of Karuna Trust described in Boxes 1.2 and 1.5 respectively. Then using the matrix below complete the SWOT diagram by noting other strengths, weaknesses, opportunities and threats.

Strengths	Weaknesses
Attractive image	Narrow funding base

Opportunities	Threats
Further cooperation with funding partners	Increased competition for funds from other organisations

One of the strengths of a SWOT diagram is that it provides a simple way of summarising the outcomes of strategic analysis. However, this strength can also be a weakness. It may oversimplify the situation. You may be uncertain about the opportunities or threats that face your organisation, or people may disagree about what your organisation's strengths and weaknesses are. So developing a strategy often means living with uncertainty, challenging cherished beliefs and working through disagreements and conflicts. As a result strategy development needs time, and periodic opportunities to get away from the day-to-day pressures of work to try to gain some sense of perspective on what you should be doing.

1.4 SUMMARY

Here is a summary of the key learning points from this session:

- Strategy sets a direction for an organisation, and brings coherence and coordination to its activities.
- Strategy goes a step further than the planning control loop, not just ensuring that targets are achieved as planned, but ensuring the targets themselves (and how they are achieved) are appropriate to the long-term purposes of the organisation and the changing needs it serves.
- The different components of an organisation's strategy are interdependent – thus an appropriate fundraising strategy will support the wider strategy of the organisation, and will itself help shape the wider strategy.
- Strategy development consists of three stages: analysis, formulation and implementation. Strategic analysis considers the relationship between an organisation and its environment.

- An organisational assessment considers the five elements of:
  mission and strategy
  resource requirements
  policies and norms
  performance
  capacities
- Mission can be summarised as what an organisation does, for whom, and how.
- Resource requirements can be divided into capital expenses, core operating costs and one-off project costs. The relative importance of each to an organisation will influence the appropriate mix of sources of support and fundraising methods.
- Organisational policies and norms help to ensure integrity, consistency, authoritative answers and coordination.
- Performance analysis considers effectiveness, efficiency, past success in fundraising and how the organisation manages its resource base.
- Organisational capacities include image, human and financial resources, systems, technology and structure.
- An organisation's environment consists of its operating environment and the macro-environment.
- The macro-environment consists of social, technological, economic and political factors also known as the STEP factors.
- The operating environment consists of the resource, decision, service and competitive domains.
- SWOT analysis (the consideration of an organisation's strengths, weaknesses, opportunities and threats) is a convenient way to bring together the different aspects of an organisational assessment and an environmental analysis.

Session 2

Thinking Strategically: Formulation and Implementation

Session 2

CONTENTS

2 THINKING STRATEGICALLY: FORMULATION AND IMPLEMENTATION

2.1 INTRODUCTION

The last session focused on the analysis phase of developing a strategy for winning resources and support. In particular it concentrated on how to assess your unit or organisation to identify its strengths and weaknesses, and how to analyse your organisation's external environment to identify new opportunities and threats it faces. In this session we will look at formulating strategy – identifying strategic options and choosing between them – and, finally, implementing strategy. Again, the purpose is to give you an appreciation of strategic thinking rather than teach the details of strategy formulation and implementation which will depend on the precise circumstances of their application.

Aims and learning outcomes

The session has three main aims:

- to describe and illustrate the different types of strategic options for winning resources and support
- to consider an approach that can be used to choose between strategic options
- to consider some of the important issues you are likely to face when implementing strategy.

After studying this session you should be able to:

- describe your own unit's or organisation's strategy for winning resources and support in terms of competitive and collaborative strategies
- identify different strategic options (both competitive and collaborative) and present reasoned arguments concerning their relevance to your own unit or organisation
- formulate criteria that could be used to assess the relative attractiveness of different strategic options in your own organisation
- use a portfolio matrix to compare and assess different strategic initiatives
- explain why an organisation's realised strategy will be an outcome of both deliberate and emergent strategies, and the implications this has for strategy formulation and implementation.

2.2 IDENTIFYING STRATEGIC OPTIONS

Broadly speaking, strategies can be divided into two sorts – competitive and collaborative. Organisations may choose to compete or cooperate with each other. However, this choice is not usually a simple one. Many organisations choose to compete in some areas and cooperate in others. Some organisations may compete for funds but cooperate in service delivery or campaigning; others may compete for service delivery but cooperate to raise funds. We will now look in more detail at some of the different ways in which voluntary and not-for-profit organisations may compete or cooperate to win resources and support.

2.2.1 Competitive strategies

There are three main ways in which an organisation can compete more effectively for resources and support:

- by doing something that is *distinctive* from other organisations
- by doing what it does *better* than other organisations, for example being more *efficient* or *effective*
- by *extending* what it does already or *innovating* to reach new sources of resources and support.

Of course, it is not just what the organisation does that is important; it is how people perceive what the organisation does that affects their decision whether to support the organisation. Sometimes this can be at variance with what the organisation itself thinks it does – so it is worth checking this out through research. Box 2.1 describes how the UK charity Guide Dogs for the Blind Association did this.

BOX 2.1

GUIDE DOGS OR PARTNERSHIPS?

Two years ago, Guide Dogs decided to invest in developing our donor base.

We assumed, because it was the case elsewhere in the world, that what would attract new supporters was to concentrate perceptions solely on 'the dog'. To our astonishment, our first mailshot based on this supposition did not do particularly well. In trying to fathom this we found that, although sector folklore had the image of the dog as our 'gold mine', what resonated with the public was the image of us creating and supporting a unique partnership.

So, taking a long, hard look at how your organisation is perceived is vital. For the past few years, Guide Dogs has been trying to build on our stakeholder research to modify some erroneous public perceptions and reinforce some key messages about our values and activities. Like many established charities, we are faced with an ageing donor base, decreasing income and an overall lack of awareness about what we do (my incredulity peaked when feedback from one piece of research showed only two per cent of people thought we bred and trained guide dogs).

Our answer was a fundamental one that lay in taking soundings from all our stakeholders, researching need and evaluating competition. Armed with this knowledge we made some real but difficult choices about what we would do in the future and what kind of organisation we wanted and needed to become.

As a result, many of our long-held assumptions about what supporters thought – about our work, how we attracted support, what methods of communication worked, even how people expected our services to be delivered – were challenged.

And this, in turn, led to new ways of working.

This has enabled us to attract a wider, more diverse audience, broaden our supporter base, develop new income streams and evolve more flexible and responsive services. We feel revitalised and our new legitimacy is infectious, attracting renewed support which could not have been attracted had we not taken that cold, hard look at ourselves

(Source: Peacock, 2003)

Developing distinctive competences

Organisations are under more competitive pressure if what they do is similar to other organisations. So organisations strive to distinguish themselves from each other in various ways. One important strategy for doing this is to specialise in a particular area, so that the organisation develops *distinctive competences* in that area and a correspondingly *distinctive image* or brand. The UK charities WaterAid and ActionAid provide good examples of this in the field of overseas development. WaterAid focuses its assistance on projects related to the supply of clean water. It also targets its fundraising on the water industry and water consumers. ActionAid targets its support on children and emphasises the link between the donor and the beneficiary of the gift. Both organisations make much of these distinctive aspects of what they do in their promotional and fundraising material.

Developing a distinctive competence is a way of trying to carve out a particular 'niche' in the environment in which to operate. For this reason they are often called *niche strategies.* Niche strategies seek to avoid direct competition by finding something distinctive and unique to do. Of course, there is no guarantee that another organisation won't attempt to develop similar competences and occupy or take over the same niche!

ACTIVITY 2.1

(a) Thinking of your organisation, or another that you know well, what do you think are the main factors that distinguish it from others working in a similar field?

(b) Does the organisation try to present a distinctive image? If so, give an example of how it does this.

(c) Do you think there are things that could usefully be done to improve the distinctiveness of your chosen organisation or its image?

Thinking about this activity from the point of view of a distance-learning business school, for example, the field of distance education is becoming more crowded but there are some distinctive features such as size, range of courses, and infrastructure which separate the OU Business School from other providers. The OU Business School certainly does try to present a distinctive image – through visual identity, public relations and other communications, and through focusing on certain areas of research which feed back into its courses. Other ways of improving the distinctiveness of the organisation need to be found continually, because of the evolving nature of the field. Perhaps emphasising the international reach of the institution, or espousing a particular model of the teaching and learning process, could set it apart from other distance-learning providers.

Efficiency and effectiveness

Another way in which organisations compete is in terms of *efficiency* and *effectiveness*. While not new, there appears to have been an increasing trend towards professionalisation and competition on the basis of efficiency. The contribution of permanent, paid staff to many voluntary organisations' efficiency is, however, something that does not always fit with donor expectations. This creates something of a paradox for effectively run organisations, some of which perhaps need to do more to make the case for professional intervention, as Stanford (2003) comments:

> Look at any survey on attitudes to voluntary-sector organisations and you will find 60 or 70 per cent questioning the need for a headquarters building, support staff, or even salaries.
>
> Hence the popularity of well-intentioned amateurs who opt to hire a lorry themselves and drive it to Romania, Ethiopia or wherever there is a humanitarian crisis, stuffed full of food and supplies collected from their neighbourhood.
>
> The reality is that administration costs are carefully managed. What is spent ensures, in the case of Romania or Ethiopia, that the aid is handled by professional staff and so gets to those who need it most, rather than falling into the hands of freeloaders who target the unsuspecting amateurs who turn up on their doorstep without a clue.
>
> (Stanford, 2003)

Of course, a charity with apparently low overheads may be classifying administrative costs under a different heading, or skimping on necessary administrative tasks such as monitoring or proper financial or resource management – which will harm its effectiveness.

It is often difficult to tell how much organisations differ in terms of efficiency and effectiveness. However, there are trends which may increase competition on the basis of some broader measures of efficiency. Perhaps the most important is the growing insistence on evaluation of organisations and their projects by funding bodies (hence the emphasis on evaluation in this course).

At a lower level, fundraisers are often trying to create an image of value for money. One way of doing this is to offer some very tangible results for money donated. For example, a conservation charity might promise to plant a tree for every pound donated. Another way of increasing perceived value for money is through what is called *leverage*. This is where the money donated is increased in proportion by another donor.

ACTIVITY 2.2

(a) Have you observed any trend towards increased professionalisation or efficiency in your own experience or reading about fundraising? Give an example.

(b) Give an example, again from your own experience or reading, of how an organisation has deliberately tried to present an image of efficiency when competing for resources or support. How relevant and/or convincing was it?

Again, answering this question from the perspective of the OU Business School, there has been a trend towards centralising functions and support services within the University as a whole in order to increase efficiency. There has also been a move to standardise systems and rationalise structures which have grown organically over the years. As far as presenting an image of efficiency is concerned, higher education in general has plenty of opportunities to do so because of the regular scrutiny to which it is subjected by quality inspections. These are complemented by accreditation by external industry bodies, many of them international.

Extending and innovating

The third way in which organisations may compete is by extending what they do to try to get support from new groups of potential supporters, or by using new methods and techniques to get more support and/or resources. A useful way of thinking about strategy in this area is to use a modified version of a popular business planning tool called Ansoff's matrix, as shown in Figure 2.1.

Target groups/audiences	Fundraising, promotional and campaigning techniques: Existing	Fundraising, promotional and campaigning techniques: New
Existing	1 Improve existing approach LEAST RISKY	2 Try out new techniques on existing supporters INTERMEDIATE RISK
New	3 Extend existing techniques to new groups INTERMEDIATE RISK	4 Try out new techniques with new groups MOST RISKY

Figure 2.1 Ways to develop your strategy for winning resources and support (Source: Ansoff, 1987)

The Ansoff matrix enables you to identify four broad options for developing strategy, where each quadrant of the matrix represents a different strategic option. These options are:

1 *Use existing techniques with existing groups of supporters/donors* – This includes the possibilities of carrying on as usual or consolidating, and trying to improve, existing approaches. For example, you might try to improve efficiency by reducing the costs of particular fundraising methods, or you might try to increase returns by improving the way a technique is used. These options have the least risk associated with them because they build on existing experience.

2 *Use new techniques on existing groups of supporters/donors* – For example, an organisation that had previously relied primarily on direct mail might introduce telephone marketing techniques to contact a selected group of existing supporters or donors.

3 *Extend the use of existing techniques to new groups* – This might be done by extending geographical coverage or targeting new groups of potential supporters and donors. For example, an organisation might open a charity shop in a new area or extend its advertising so that it reaches new groups of potential supporters.

4 *Try out new techniques with new groups* – For example, a number of charities in the UK have adopted face-to-face street solicitation as a new method of fundraising effective for reaching new groups of younger donors. The investment involved in such approaches is considerable – which increases the risk – and at least one organisation specialising in the service has gone bankrupt since its launch in the UK (Maggs, 2002).

ACTIVITY 2.3

To 'get inside' the Ansoff Matrix, draw on your experience of your own organisation, or other organisations that you are familiar with, to give examples of the four different options for developing new ways of winning resources or support.

Improving existing approaches:

New techniques with existing donors/supporters:

Extending existing techniques to new groups:

New techniques with new groups:

A business school like the OU Business School raises funds in a number of ways. The OU Affinity Card is a successful initiative aimed at current and past students. New techniques with existing donors and supporters include a legacy campaign. Extending existing techniques to new groups is problematic, because the mainstay of any university's constituency is likely to remain those who have been touched by its activities. However, as the organisation internationalises, this presents the opportunity to address new groups of students and alumni along national lines. Finally, bringing new techniques to new audiences might involve a greater emphasis on tapping new veins of corporate support by innovative projects involving elements of research and consultancy alongside philanthropic giving.

2.2.2 Collaborative strategies

The danger of thinking only in terms of competition when formulating strategy is that the possibilities of collaborative strategies will be overlooked. Cooperation is one way in which organisations can try to gain more power over their environment and enables them to do things that by themselves would be too difficult or risky. A good example in the area of fundraising is the way that various charities join together to help promote and sell Christmas cards. Costs, risks and rewards of the operation are shared between the organisations (though it is a very tough market because of the external competition such consortia face from commercial operations).

A disadvantage of collaborative strategies is that they inevitably involve the organisation in some loss of autonomy – agreements have to be reached with other organisations about what goals and methods to pursue. The greater the degree of cooperation, the more individual organisations may have to negotiate and make compromises about their own distinctive values and goals. In addition, collaboration may pose a threat to an organisation's distinctive identity. This tension between greater power to overcome environmental and organisational constraints versus loss of autonomy and identity is often at the heart of any decisions concerning cooperative strategies.

Cooperative strategies can be subdivided into two broad types – what we can call *vertical* collaboration and *horizontal* collaboration. Vertical collaboration in this context involves collaboration between an organisation and its funders, or between an organisation and those who receive resources from it. Such collaboration is usually oriented around the provision of services and is often known as a *partnership* arrangement. For example, a local health authority may provide funds to a voluntary organisation to provide a particular welfare service, or an organisation like Oxfam may give funds to a smaller agency to develop particular projects. This type of collaboration over the provision of services often involves competition between similar organisations for resources. Funders usually have limited resources for particular initiatives, and grants and contracts are often awarded on a competitive basis. As a result, from a perspective of winning resources, vertical collaboration can be treated as creating potential competition, and the different ways of competing described earlier apply to this situation (particularly in the drive towards efficiency and effectiveness).

Horizontal collaboration involves similar organisations collaborating to provide a common service, to run a campaign or to acquire resources that will benefit them both. This type of collaboration may take three broad forms – joint projects, alliances and coalitions, and mergers. We will look at each of these options in more detail, and highlight some of the questions and issues that you will need to consider when thinking about the relevance of these strategies for winning resources and support in your own organisation.

Joint projects between similar organisations

Joint projects come in all shapes and sizes, from informal agreements on sharing information and resources, to contractual relationships between organisations, to the establishment of consortia. Some of the better known joint projects are the consortia that have been set up by a number of charities to promote joint trading catalogues, Christmas cards, and joint collections.

The main reason for setting up joint projects is that it allows participating organisations to achieve things they would find difficult on their own. The basis for cooperation is that each organisation has something to offer the project. The advantage to participating organisations is that they can share any risks and reduce the need for each one to acquire all the necessary skills and resources to carry out the work themselves. However, they may need to develop new management structures and new skills in managing such projects, otherwise lines of responsibility may become hopelessly tangled between the different organisations. Another advantage is that the project puts a fairly clear boundary on the extent of cooperation.

Even though joint working seems to make sense, as Box 2.2 illustrates, it can nevertheless raise a number of questions. How should joint projects be managed? How are responsibilities to be allocated and reporting lines set up? What about the finances of the project – will a separate bank account and set of accounts be necessary? What impact will the new initiative have on the other work of the organisations? How will the various identities of the participating organisations be preserved in any public relations or campaigning work associated with the project? Joint ventures are formed for a specific purpose, but often have trouble maintaining stability in the longer term. For this reason it is not a strategy that should be embarked upon without a good deal of thought and planning. In particular it is important that the organisations concerned work out some agreement on how responsibilities will be shared between them, and how the project will be managed and controlled. If the project is small a letter of agreement between the two organisations may be sufficient. A larger initiative may require a more formal agreement.

BOX 2.2

OUT OF THE PUDDLE

In a tight funding environment, it makes sense to work together. Yet the general rule amongst charities – of which there are almost 200,000 in the UK alone – is of intense competition for the limited resources available. No wonder the charity sector has been called a 'shark-filled puddle'.

Yet the Ealing Community Resource Centre in West London is one of a number of initiatives which show that charities can work together successfully to share resources. The centre's shared spaces and facilities have been specially designed to encourage cooperation between users, aiming to maximise their ability to learn from each other and network effectively. Built as part of a £10 million development which includes 36 affordable homes, the centre cost £650,000 to fit out. Funding was provided by Capacitybuilders, the Big Lottery Fund, the local council and a number of local businesses. Thus even the funding of the centre has a collaborative flavour.

(Source: based on Jump, 2007)

ACTIVITY 2.4

(a) Thinking of your own organisation, or another with which you are familiar, does it engage in any joint projects for winning resources or support? If so, list them below.

(b) Can you identify any other areas where you feel that there might be potential for joint projects which could help the organisation secure more resources or support?

(c) What do you think are likely to be the main advantages and disadvantages of joint projects? Give examples from your own experience if possible.

Advantages:

Disadvantages:

Some possible advantages of undertaking joint projects are:

- *it allows organisations to do things that they would find difficult to do individually*
- *it spreads the risks*
- *it can enhance credibility in the eyes of funders.*

Some possible disadvantages of undertaking joint projects are:

- *it can cause management problems*
- *the participating organisations might lose their individual identities*
- *there is a danger that the two organisations might pull the project in different directions.*

Alliances and coalitions

Alliances and coalitions move beyond the fairly clearly defined boundaries of joint projects – they tend to be issue-based rather than project-based. They have the advantage of strength through numbers – allowing a range of organisations to work together to pursue common goals and interests. One of the strengths of the year-long debt relief campaign run for the UK in 2005 was the sheer diversity of its 540 member organisations (Shimmin and Coles, 2007, p. 32).

Alliances and coalitions provide a framework for organisations to explore how they can best work together to tackle particular issues. As a result, they are more likely to raise issues which challenge the values, goals and autonomy of member organisations than strategies involving joint projects. For example, coalitions concerned with disability have raised serious and challenging questions about the policies and practices of many of the traditional agencies which provide services to people with disabilities. Consequently any decisions to form alliances should not be taken lightly.

ACTIVITY 2.5

(a) Again, thinking of your own organisation or another which you know well, are there any areas of winning resources and support where you feel it might benefit from pursuing strategic alliances or coalitions?

(b) If yes, choose one area and list below what you think some of the main advantages might be, and any difficulties or problems you think might arise in pursuing such an option.

Advantages:

Problems/difficulties:

Probably the main advantage is that several organisations together are likely to have more influence than they do separately. Another possible advantage is that organisations will be in a good position to learn from each other.

Some possible problems are: an organisation might not want to be identified with everything the coalition does; there may be conflicts of interest and competition between organisations; getting common agreement might slow progress down, or lead to proposals being 'watered down'.

Mergers

A voluntary merger between organisations, as opposed to a take-over of one organisation by another, is an example of taking a cooperative strategy to its limits. The reason for mergers is usually to achieve greater economies of scale and greater influence than either organisation could obtain individually. There is an additional pressure on charities with apparently similar aims and services to merge because of public perceptions of inefficient duplication. This view is shared by Victor Adebowale, chief executive of drugs charity Turning Point and the chair of a UK government task group which investigated cooperation between charities: 'I take exception to the view of the voluntary sector as a thousand flowers blooming. You end up wasting a lot of fertiliser' (Little, 2003). Mergers among voluntary organisations and charities are still relatively rare but becoming more common. The barriers to joint projects between peer organisations, mentioned above, also militate against mergers.

In addition, unlike companies, voluntary organisations and charities do not have shareholders with an overriding material interest to determine such decisions and overcome the inevitable conflicts of loyalties, interests, values and egos. The legal constraints on charities also make mergers difficult, although they can be spectacularly successful. The combination of two cancer charities in the UK (Imperial Cancer Research and the Cancer Research Campaign) led to a 12 per cent increase in its fundraising income in its first year as Cancer Research UK (Kelly, 2003a).

While this is impressive, there are other voices in the merger debate which counsel against the creation of what may turn out to be monolithic bureaucracies at odds with the pioneering, nimble-footed traditions of smaller charities. Peter Cardy, chief executive of the UK's Macmillan Cancer Relief charity, puts it like this: 'The proliferation of cancer charities is always represented as a bad thing. But if you take a walk down a busy High Street you don't hear people complaining that there are too many shops selling similar things. People like it that there are different brands with different packaging so that they can pick which is best for them' (Kelly, 2003b). Fundraisers need to know where their donors are likely to stand on the issue of mergers, and be able to justify their organisation's policy if a strategic decision has been taken to remain independent in the face of a potential merger.

2.3 DEVELOPING AND CHOOSING STRATEGIC OPTIONS

So far we have looked at a range of possible strategic options. The options that your organisation chooses to develop may be competitive or collaborative or some combination of different options. This choice should be based on a careful assessment of your organisation's strengths and weaknesses and the opportunities and threats it faces from a changing environment. We can illustrate this point by returning to the example of Karuna Trust. Box 2.3 shows how the options that were developed stemmed from the organisational assessment and environmental analysis that were carried out.

BOX 2.3

STRATEGIC OPTIONS AT KARUNA TRUST

Karuna has developed its strategy over time to meet the varied changes in its external environment by adapting to circumstances, but always keeping within its Buddhist principles and its mission of working to alleviate the poverty of the poorest communities.

It has progressively broadened its mix of sources of funds and fundraising techniques from purely door-to-door work, to seek funds from charitable trusts and institutional funders, then through its partners from Taiwan. It is now considering fundraising in India itself, and possibly broadening its range of fundraising techniques in the UK.

Karuna dealt with the problems of growth and accountability by moving away from working through one organisation in India, to taking on several partners, thus lowering the risk to its operations from any one partner. Its work now spreads over five states and it acquires greater knowledge of the management and progress of the projects it funds. As with any family, this took time and tact, but the process was galvanised by a family crisis, which could only be properly addressed by agreed changes in practice.

Karuna could engage with other communities outside India. For example, it could look at the possibilities of working with people in or from Nepal, Burma or Thailand and position its most popular projects as flagships in its fundraising programme.

It could also reconsider the flow of money and direction of management from West to East and establish branches of supporters in say, Taiwan, Hong Kong, Singapore and India who would raise funds and perhaps take part in the wider political process of setting policy and direction for the organisation.

A source of concern is that as Karuna loses or lessens its unique and significant source of income from door-to-door fundraising it is vulnerable to competition for funds from other larger and better-known development organisations. It remains to be seen if its immersion in Buddhism and/or its knowledge of how to deliver effective programmes on the ground will give it an adequate edge over the competition in the long term.

If you work for a small organisation like Karuna Trust your strategy may focus on developing a small number of initiatives for winning resources and support. However, if you work in a large organisation you may develop a much wider range of initiatives. In this situation it is particularly useful to have a way of looking at the range of initiatives and make sure that you have some sort of balance between them. An approach that has been developed in the business world for doing this is called *portfolio analysis*. The essence of this approach is to look at the financial health of a collection of businesses or products, and is analogous to the 'investment portfolio' a shareholder might seek to assemble in order to hold a balanced range of shares. The aim of portfolio analysis is to look at the *contribution* of each business and product, and the demands or costs involved, so that it can be decided which should be developed and which should be dropped or sold off.

A variety of techniques has been developed for portfolio analysis, which tries to assess the relative attractiveness of developing various businesses or products. These techniques cannot always be adopted directly by not-for-profit organisations because, unlike in businesses, resource acquisition is usually separated from service delivery. Nevertheless, in many cases they can be adapted to provide useful analytical tools.

The 'portfolio matrix' we are going to introduce here is adapted from a technique developed by the General Electric Company in 1970s America, and is usually called the GE matrix. The two dimensions of the portfolio matrix are the *external attractiveness* and *internal appropriateness* of the activities or initiatives, as shown in Figure 2.2.

The external attractiveness of an initiative or activity concerns its capacity to attract resources and support. This may be judged by combining a number of different assessments, which might include the level of public concern or support, likely trends in public

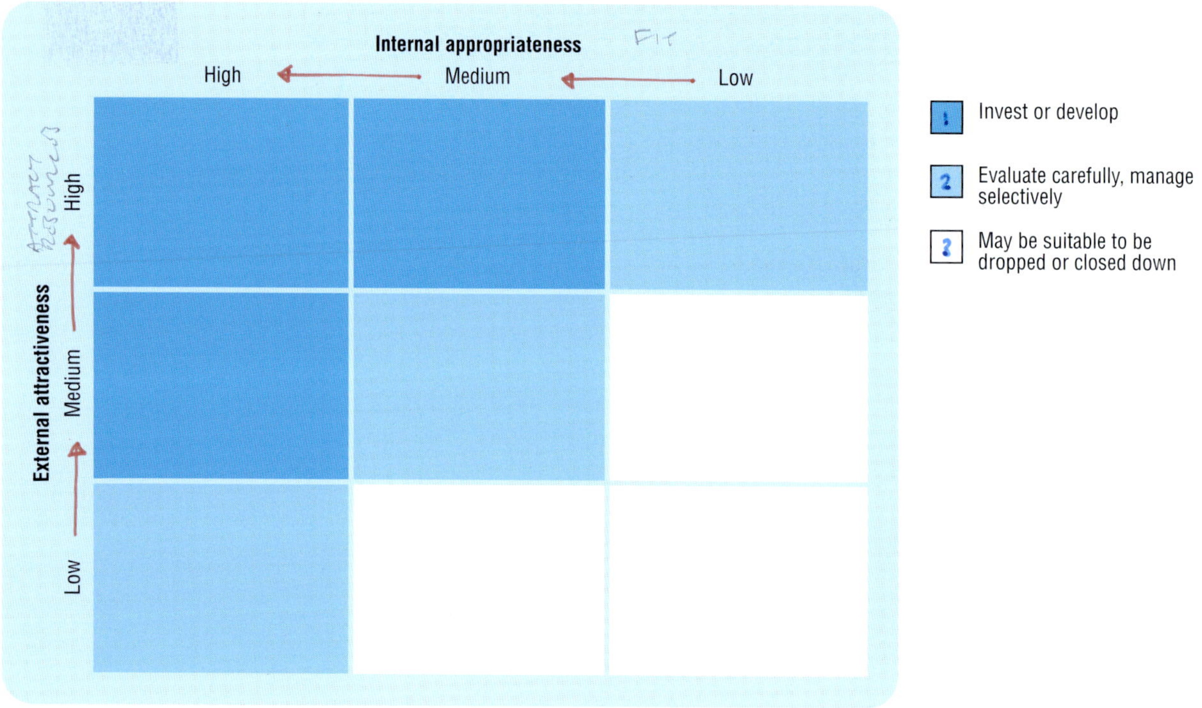

Figure 2.2 A portfolio matrix (Source: Dittrich, 1988)

concern, the capacity to attract funds and/or to attract volunteers, members or donations in kind, and indirect benefits such as publicity. It is up to those involved to specify this dimension in a way that is appropriate to the circumstances they face. While it is true that donors give to causes rather than to fundraising schemes, some schemes are likely to be more attractive than others. We have argued elsewhere that fundraising initiatives such as events have 'life-cycles' – suggesting that spotting a popular trend early enough may confer an advantage on those organisations enterprising enough to innovate. Ease of participation, fun and convenience are all characteristics associated with external attractiveness. The internal appropriateness of an initiative concerns the extent to which it 'fits' the organisation. A number of different factors may be used to assess this: compatibility with the organisation's mission and values, its feasibility given the resources available, how well the initiative fits with other activities the organisation is pursuing, how acceptable it is likely to be to members of the organisation, how well it contributes to the organisation's mix of initiatives to raise resources, and so on. An example might help here. Legacy fundraising, for instance, may be more or less appropriate to a particular organisation for a number of reasons: the characteristics of the existing donor community, the urgency of the need to be met (given that such campaigns take time to bear fruit) and the resources and contacts of the organisation itself.

The environmental and organisational assessment that you were introduced to in the last session should provide you with information to help you judge the external attractiveness and internal appropriateness of particular initiatives.

ACTIVITY 2.6

Can you think of some criteria that an organisation of your choice might want to use to help assess the external attractiveness and internal appropriateness of different strategic initiatives for winning resources or support?

Criteria for external attractiveness:

Criteria for internal appropriateness:

For a business school such criteria might include:

- *external: the relevance of the initiative to the issues and interests of supporters at a particular time (e.g. setting up a scholarship fund in memory of a particular individual who has been connected in some way with the institution)*
- *internal: the strategic direction of research and teaching developments which need support, the ease with which the initiative could be run using existing expertise and systems.*

No doubt you will have plenty of other criteria relevant to the particular supporters and organisation you have chosen as the subject of the Activity.

The portfolio matrix can be divided into three areas, as shown in Figure 2.2. Each initiative being considered is judged using agreed criteria, like those outlined above, and placed in an appropriate box in the matrix. Initiatives that are placed in the top left-hand corner of the matrix are obvious candidates for development, as they are judged appropriate for the organisation and likely to be attractive externally to potential funders and supporters. Those initiatives following in the diagonal area need to be considered carefully and each will have to be judged on its merits. For example, if an initiative is highly appropriate for the organisation you may decide it worth going ahead with, even though the chances of attracting external support are small. It may be worth considering what scope there is for improving the initiative's position. Initiatives in the bottom right-hand corner have to be seriously reviewed. If they cannot be reoriented or reorganised to improve their position, and if they are using valuable resources that could be redirected to other initiatives, they are obvious candidates to be dropped or closed down.

Hence the technique of portfolio analysis provides a framework for *comparing* and *choosing between* different initiatives that will make up a strategy. However, it should be remembered that following an approach like this is not a guarantee of success. The approach involves a number of difficult judgements, and the outcome will only be as good as the judgements made. For example, you may have over-estimated the likely attractiveness of an initiative to potential donors and supporters, or you may have underestimated the costs and expertise required and so misjudged its internal appropriateness.

ACTIVITY 2.7

Consider three different initiatives that your organisation (or another one with which you are familiar) has, or is considering developing, to win resources and support. Use your own judgement to place them on the portfolio matrix shown below. What conclusions do you draw from this about the sustainability of the initiatives?

		Internal appropriateness		
		High	Medium	Low
External Attractiveness	High			
	Medium			
	Low			

You can use this rough-and-ready portfolio matrix for two purposes. First, it can help you think through what strategy your organisation should be adopting to win resources and support:

- *What initiatives are most likely to win high external support?*
- *Are these initiatives internally appropriate?*
- *If not, can they be reoriented to improve their appropriateness?*
- *What initiatives are most appropriate internally?*
- *Are they likely to attract external support?*
- *If not, can they be modified to improve attractiveness?*
- *What resources will the initiatives require?*
- *Can they all be developed at once?*
- *Do they give the resources necessary for the organisation to fulfil its goals for service development and delivery?*

Second, you can use the matrix as a basis for discussion with others:

- *Do they agree with where you have placed initiatives on the matrix?*
- *On what basis have different people made their judgements?*
- *How far can these judgements be relied upon – where do you need to do more in-depth research?*

Such discussions may allow possible divisions between groups such as fundraisers and service providers to be opened up and addressed.

2.4 IMPLEMENTING STRATEGY

'...before you judge the brilliance of your written strategy, don't forget that, as Thomas Edison might have said, a successful strategy is one per cent inspiration and ninety-nine per cent implementation.'

(Source: Giles Pegram, Appeals Director and Deputy Chief Executive NSPCC, in Mullen, 2002, p. 114)

As we have seen, strategy is the highest level of planning. It is about sorting out the overall direction and long-term goals for a unit or an organisation. Once your organisation's strategic options for winning resources and support have been decided they will need to be implemented. Implementation requires more planning – plans will need to be made for how the various initiatives and activities that make up the strategy can be put into effect. Rather than reiterating detail covered elsewhere about the cycle of analysis, planning, implementation and review, we will begin this consideration of strategy implementation with some reflections on issues which may affect, or even prevent, its fulfilment. These are:

- resistance to change
- tension between deliberate and emergent strategy
- power
- priorities.

Resistance to change

Frequently a new strategy will require an organisation to make changes – to embrace new goals, start new activities and perhaps drop others, use resources in different ways, and so on. This will require at least some members of the organisation to make changes. Experience shows that bringing about change is frequently a complex and difficult process. People often resist change – the proposed change may not agree with their view of the

The consequences of delay, confusion and demotivation of potential donors threaten the success of the plan itself. You may be able to relate this to your own experience or wider reading. In a capital appeal, for example, a carefully phased strategy of approaching major donors, selected trusts and, finally, the community appeal, needs to be carefully kept to. There might be the temptation for senior management, impatient with apparent lack of progress and acutely conscious of the need to deliver, to demand short-term action which will hamper long-term effectiveness. As with the issues around change management discussed earlier, a way forward lies in the kind of techniques available for managing external support. Internal communications and trust-building are as important in implementing plans as external communications and relationship management are in resourcing them. Objectives have to be specific, measurable, agreed, realistic and time-limited – but they also need to be made somebody's responsibility. Agreeing, and accepting, the resulting delegation of authority is an essential part of successful implementation. Contingency planning needs to be agreed and included in this, rather than becoming vulnerable to short-term, poorly planned bursts of counterproductive activity.

The final difficulty facing implementation is one of priorities. The same anonymous writer comments:

> An organisation cannot make the implementation of a strategy a priority simply by saying that this is the case. This trap has been a major problem in this strategy implementation. The strategy is presented to the external participants as the key and major programme for the organisation, but internally other issues are allowed to divert attention and resource. The fact that the individuals who commissioned the development of the strategy are informed is not enough – unless they are prepared to make the time, to dedicate the resources, to follow the timetable plan and to play the role allocated to them, the strategy will again falter and stall.

(Quoted in Mullin, 2002)

Although this appears to be describing a situation where an external strategy has been commissioned by an organisation to deal with a specific campaign or appeal, the same principle of necessary ownership applies to any internally devised fundraising strategy. Unless the organisation is prepared to prioritise the implementation of a plan it will remain unachieved. There is a parallel with the danger of spending so much time and resource on perfecting a plan that it becomes an end in itself rather than a means to an end. A good strategy, like a good case statement, should reach beyond the institution to the wider environment. This acts as a 'reality check' and helps ground the strategy in a practical sense of what is possible given the organisation's size, resources and ongoing commitments. Otherwise, as in the example cited above, the strategy can get stuck in the realms of wishful thinking.

The key to avoiding this situation lies in thorough analysis using the SWOT and STEP models we have reviewed in this book. These models are not abstract checklists, but tools to ensure that the fullest picture is available of an organisation's capabilities and weaknesses, and of the possible constraints acting on it. Some assumptions are necessary in any analysis, but the virtue of a comprehensive SWOT and STEP approach is that it compels you to consider areas of the organisation and its environment that might otherwise be taken for granted. This forces you to acknowledge and question the assumptions you might make in the absence of information or evidence, reducing the likelihood of being taken by surprise if the organisation's real priorities are different from those espoused in the strategy. It might be, for example, that the organisation desperately wants to move forward into a new project attracted by the perceived urgency of need, but is actually expanding too quickly to be able to concentrate on the necessary resource-winning work given its commitments to its current operations. As with the Karuna Trust in the 1990s (Box 1.2), the better way forward might be consolidation and an organisational rethink, rather than expansion into yet more new projects based on an unsustainable organisational model.

ACTIVITY 2.8

(a) Thinking about your organisation, or another which you know well, does it have a strategic plan for winning resources and support? If so, are there aspects of this that have not been implemented or not implemented as originally intended?

(b) Are there aspects of your chosen organisation's realised strategy that have emerged rather than been deliberately planned? If so, give an example.

Answering this question fully might require you to have a good deal of inside knowledge about your chosen organisation's plans and history. But here is an example, from personal experience, of how a planned strategy changed in the light of an emerging one.

A regional theatre wanted to launch a scheme to encourage committed giving from local businesses. The original strategy had been to recruit businesses by offering corporate membership at a number of levels (to which were attached a tiered set of benefits). Feedback from early members, however, suggested that the main motivation for local businesses to join was less to do with being seen to be good corporate citizens, and more to do with entertainment opportunities to impress clients at a prestigious venue. Furthermore, the theatre's development staff had discovered that they could make significant amounts of extra money by selling additional items, like branded merchandise, to members for use as business gifts to their guests on top of the advertised package. The scheme was relaunched two years later with a much simpler membership structure, but with a great deal more scope for negotiation by the development department. What had started life as a strategy to maximise income by offering different but ***fixed grades of association*** *with the theatre, developed into a new (and very successful)* ***strategy of flexible negotiation with individual clients****. The strategy that emerged was partly due to the real nature of demand revealing itself, but also due to the enterprising approach of the development staff.*

2.5 SUMMARY

Here is a summary of the main learning points from this session:

- Strategies fall into two types: competitive and collaborative (though organisations can deploy a mixture of such strategies).
- Competitive strategy consists of either:

  doing something distinctive (e.g. clear branding or niche positioning)

  doing something better (e.g. concentrating on efficiency or effectiveness)

  doing something new (e.g. extending and innovating).
- Ansoff's matrix (1987) is a useful way to clarify strategic thinking on the risks and rewards from the combination of new or existing fundraising techniques with new or existing donor groups.
- Collaborative strategies allow organisations to exert more power over their environments than they could achieve individually while sharing risks, but at the cost of sacrificing autonomy and identity.
- Vertical collaboration involves collaboration between an organisation and its funders, or those whom it benefits (e.g. the provision of resources by a development agency to a local group for its own fundraising work).
- Horizontal collaboration involves similar organisations collaborating to provide a common service, such as running a joint campaign.

- Horizontal collaboration can take the form of joint projects, coalitions around particular issues, and mergers.
- The portfolio matrix can be used to help select from a choice of strategies by balancing their internal appropriateness to an organisation with their external attractiveness to donors and supporters.
- Strategy implementation can be delayed or prevented by:

  resistance to change

  tension between deliberate and emergent strategy

  power struggles

  different priorities in an organisation.
- Mintzberg (1987) differentiates between deliberate strategy (that which is intended) and emergent strategy (that which happens as a response to the unexpected). Their combination produces realised strategy.

Session 3

The Competent Resource Winner: Reviewing Your Learning

Session 3

CONTENTS

1 THE COMPETENT RESOURCE WINNER: REVIEWING YOUR LEARNING

3.1 INTRODUCTION

It is time to look back and remind yourself of the ground you have covered. And also to pause and reflect on what it all means and what you do with it, now that, in some sense, you have it all.

Any course has to divide up its material into a series of separate topics. But however this is done, the separate topics are not really so separate after all. In real life aspects of, say, donor development will be relevant to participative fundraising or campaigning, or to formulating a longer-term strategy. Likewise, your understanding of different types of supporter and the best ways of appealing to them will be grounded in your ability to acquire, manage and use information. Indeed, as the course has progressed, you have probably noticed (and made) more and more margin notes linking back to reinforce points or develop ideas that had earlier been considered in a different context or perspective.

So, reviewing the course, and considering what you have gained from it, involves more than just looking back over the 20 or so study sessions. It also involves integrating and tying together material from different study sessions, from items on the website or online discussions, from supplementary readings or from tutorials or day schools. It is about the big picture as much as particular issues or techniques. To get the most out of this sort of course, you have to make the connections between different ideas and experiences, so that, faced with a particular instance, you can bring to bear a wide range of perspectives, techniques and concepts. In this way, you can develop a rounded view and can act with confidence. So the aim of this session is not just to help you recall the different topics the course has considered. More importantly, its aims are to tie things together, to highlight some of the connections between the different aspects of winning resources and support that you have been considering, and to give you a helicopter view of the territory you have been exploring on the ground.

Aims and learning outcomes

In particular the session aims:

- to provide a framework within which you can review your learning from the course
- to revisit your application of concepts and models to your own organisation and its approach to winning resources

- to revisit your assessment of your own professional practice and competence in Session 1, Book 1.

After studying this session you should be able to:

- review your learning from the course
- review your application of concepts and models to your own organisation and its approach to winning resources
- review your assessment of your own professional practice and competence
- identify your further development needs and opportunities, and plan appropriately to meet them.

3.2 REVIEWING YOUR LEARNING

How can we tie it all together? What are the key threads that connect up the activities of, say, the overseas aid worker trying to raise funds to assist those affected by disasters and emergencies, the Muslim group trying to raise money from their community to support a youth project, the university alumni officer and the person designing a direct mail pack for a national charity? Throughout the course you have been studying the subject of winning resources and support in two broad ways. The first has involved you in learning about the generic topics of strategy, communications and evaluation, and the range of issues and options involved in the different methods of fundraising aimed at, respectively, individuals, large numbers of people, and institutions. These we call the 'three pillars of fundraising' and the following section will use this concept to show how the different aspects of fundraising link together.

Knowing *about* fundraising and campaigning is not quite the same, however, as knowing *how* to win resources and support in practice. The second focus of your study has been the practical development of a wide range of skills and competences which you need in order to be an effective and successful practitioner. These may be things that you have been picking up for yourself through the activities, reflection on your own situation, the exercises you have done, and so forth. Here we will set out some activities you may undertake to reflect on how you can now reinforce and extend the competences you have developed through the course. Let us turn now to the three pillars of fundraising.

3.2.1 The three pillars of fundraising

This section provides a map of the territory – a 'helicopter view' of the main ways in which organisations can set about winning resources and support, and the way that the key concepts of organisational image, ethics, communication and strategy underpin these, leading to the results you seek. The territory will be familiar to you already. The simplest way of distinguishing different ways of winning support is in terms of *who* is being asked and *how*.

Are you asking individuals face to face? Or indirectly, through the media or by letter? Or are you approaching institutions rather than individuals? These three broad possibilities are represented in Figure 3.1 as pillars that support the organisation's services and achievements, and that rest upon its public reputation and the awareness of its cause.

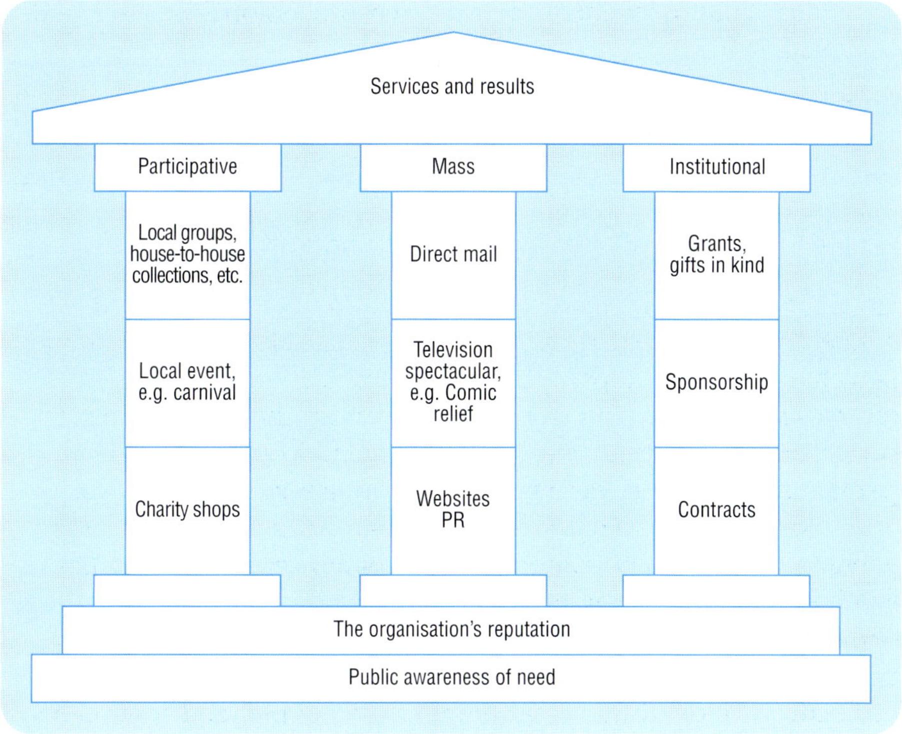

Figure 3.1 The three pillars of fundraising

The first pillar covers what we will call *participative* fundraising and campaigning. It includes many of the traditional, people-intensive methods of winning support. Hence the key skills are those of *organising* people and events. Usually this family of methods achieves results through large numbers of modest contributions or actions. The contribution multiplier that you met in Book 3 showed how many small inputs can multiply and lead to, in some cases, very substantial results. However, participative approaches are also used to attract more substantial personal contributions from a smaller number of relatively wealthy or powerful people through networking and personal solicitation.

The second pillar uses the media and the internet to interest and appeal to large, remote, distributed audiences. It could be called impersonal (instead of *mass*) fundraising and campaigning – but its practitioners claim this approach can and should be personal. The key skills here are *communication*, especially through the media, and *information management*.

The third pillar is *institutional* fundraising and campaigning – and again this is a time-honoured approach that has existed for as long as there have been governments, companies, trusts and other powerful organisations with resources, decisions and influence to dispense. *Lobbying*, *networking* and *negotiating* become particularly important in this context.

Two points about this classification are important. First, like most of its kind, the classification does not work perfectly. Some methods do not fit easily into one pillar only – for example, personal solicitation of a big gift from a wealthy individual would probably be classified as participative fundraising because it is face to face with a private individual, but in some ways it is like seeking a grant from a particular sort of institution. Nevertheless, as a broad overview of the territory, you will find the three pillars helpful. This way of dividing up the subject has some limitations, however. All of the different skills required by fundraisers and campaigners are still likely to be needed in the approaches in each of the pillars – it is only their relative importance that varies.

ACTIVITY 3.1

Spend five minutes considering the following questions:

(a) Which of these pillars does your fundraising experience most reflect?

(b) Can you think of other methods that do not fall easily into one or other of the pillars?

Many of these methods in the different pillars are used together as part of an integrated campaign – for example, the mass advertising methods used by many charities to support participative events. Another method that does not fit easily into this scheme is attracting legacies: this often uses mass methods of information analysis to identify prospects, but the 'ask' itself may be done face to face.

All these methods are built on the solid foundations you laid in the issues you studied in Books 1, 2 and 5, and earlier in this book: thinking about the strategies needed to make your fundraising case; how to communicate this including the reputation of your organisation; how to manage these processes including people, information and finance; and then ultimately how this links back into evaluation and strategy. Figure 3.2 is one way of thinking about how all the different aspects of the course link together. You may find this useful in preparing for the examination.

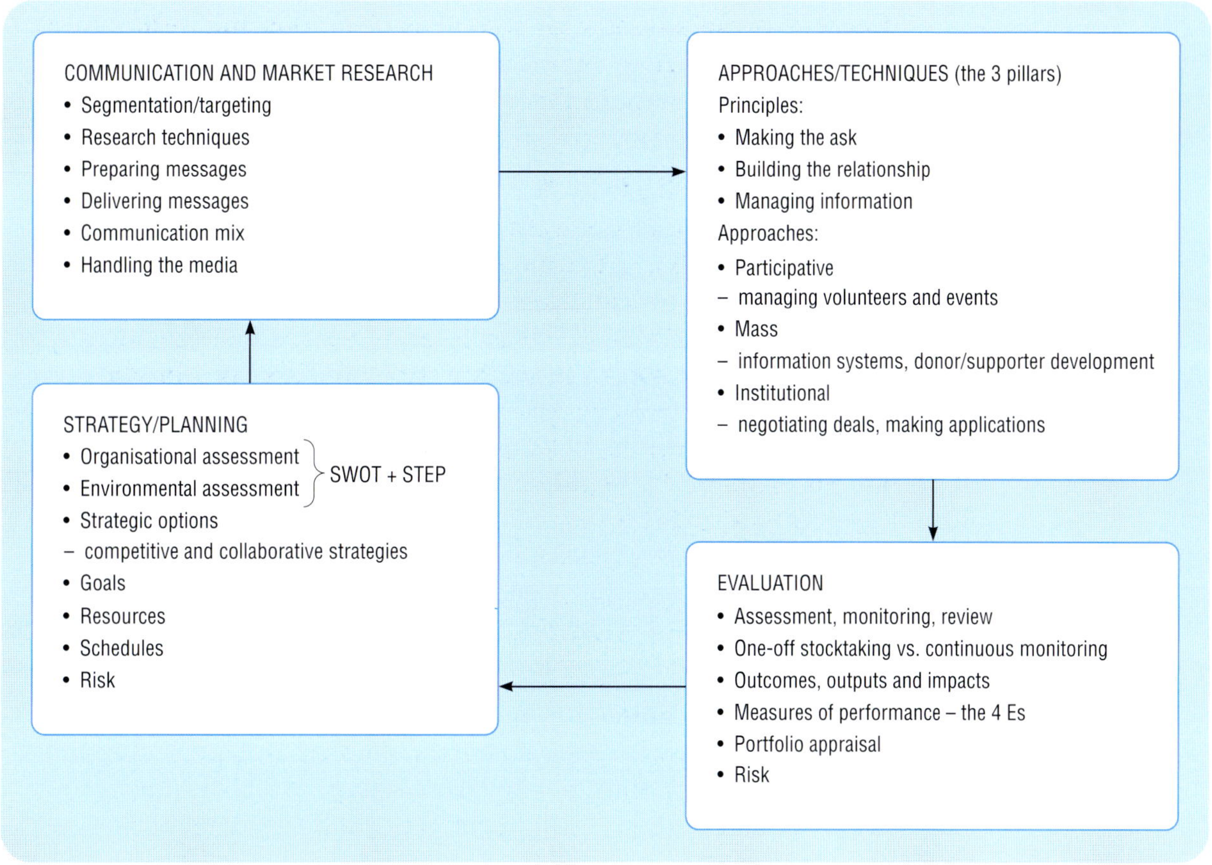

Figure 3.2 The course framework

3.2.2 Competences revisited

As we stated earlier, the issue in fundraising is more than simply knowing all the theories about how to do it. It is about being able to put these into practice and being successful at bringing much-needed resources into your organisation. To that end, we want to return to where the course began, by considering the roles and competences involved in winning resources and support. In doing so, we will develop the earlier discussion, building on the material you have studied since then, and relating it to other aspects of managerial and organisational work. This recasting of roles and competences will not only help you reflect actively and critically on what you have learned. It will also suggest ways in which the particular skills and competences you have developed relate to frameworks of professional skills, knowledge and competence, such as vocational qualifications (including the Institute of Fundraising's Certificate in Fundraising Management to which this course is an accredited path).

One problem of looking at what you do in terms of competences is that they tend to fragment work into a range of discrete activities. The danger is that you can easily lose sight of how these competences contribute to the overall task you face. One way of overcoming this fragmentation is to group competences in terms of how they contribute to key roles that have to be fulfilled. This course has tried to develop your capacities in relation to three key roles that are fundamental to work in this area – your role as a *strategist and planner*, as a *communicator*, and as a *manager* of particular fundraising, campaigning and promotional activities. Examining the competences that are required for these three key roles, we can see how the different materials in the course contribute towards winning resources and support.

The role of *strategist and planner* requires that you are able to:

1 Plan, implement and review particular events, appeals and campaigns.

The strategy may be for the whole of your organisation, or for the parts of it for which you are responsible. This may involve gathering, sharing and analysing information about internal and external developments, and working with others in the organisation to define a feasible and desirable future that fits with the organisation's mission and values.

It may, therefore, involve representing the concerns of the resource-acquisition function within wider policy debates. It will certainly mean being abreast of developments in a fast-moving field. It involves taking account of the human, financial and other resources available, as well as trends affecting potential supporters. Implementing any strategies involves setting objectives and planning, and perhaps the integration of different approaches, or of national and local activities. It means knowing how to monitor progress, and being able to use that information to learn and adapt.

The role of *communicator* means that you must be able to:

2 Communicate effectively with a variety of external and internal audiences.

This means being able to recognise the different audiences you may need to address and their different motivations for supporting you, to define and express clearly the message you want to put across, and to choose and use different media to fit the circumstances. It may mean 'making the ask' personally or in writing – or arranging for this to be done in the most effective way possible by other people.

The role of *manager* of particular fundraising, campaigning and promotional activities means that you must be able to:

3 Manage staff and volunteers.

This involves finding and working with the active supporters and supporters' groups who undertake community fundraising, or who help on campaign or appeal committees; it involves recognising the different roles you may need to adopt in relation to leading supporters and the different ways in which supporters can contribute.

4 Collect, analyse and manage relevant information.

This covers all aspects of an organisation's information use for winning resources and support, not just its list or database of supporters, members or donors. It requires an appreciation of the value of information for the coordination of activities, and of record keeping for the monitoring and review of activities, campaigns and events. It also involves an appreciation of the specialist information and services that are available to support fundraising and campaigning.

5 Develop and maintain effective relations with donors, supporters and other relevant agencies.

This involves listening to and responding to donors, members, supporters, funders and other key stakeholders. It may involve understanding motivations, developing and sustaining commitment, and delivering on expectations. It may also involve arranging the occasions, visits or telephone calls that will affirm the value that your organisation places on particular relationships, making it part of your role as communicator as well as manager.

6 Deal effectively with the commercial aspects of winning resources and support.

This involves basic financial knowledge and skills, including the ability to cost and appraise projects, to use budgets and to calculate returns. It may also involve negotiating contracts with suppliers, agents or consultants, pricing services and assessing commercial risks – or at least contributing to decisions about these matters.

7 Choose and apply as appropriate various approaches or techniques for winning resources and support.

This means being familiar with a range of different techniques and approaches and being able to make things happen, and happen well. This is what Book l referred to as 'practitioner know-how'. The particular activities and events which are important for you will depend on your context. You might need to know about house-to-house collections, abseiling down the church steeple, running a charity shop and getting the annual report out – or a quite different and longer list of particular activities and methods. The competent fundraiser is familiar with a reasonable range of activities – but no one has direct experience of running all of them, by any means. It also involves monitoring and evaluating activities, dealing with problems, making recommendations for improvements or new developments and implementing agreed changes.

So, people in the business of winning resources and support have to be strategists and planners, communicators, and managers of particular sorts of relationships, activities and events. And while this is simply a statement of roles and competences introduced in Book 1, it is now possible to consider how the different topics in the course all relate back to these three key roles and seven basic competences.

ACTIVITY 3.2

How do the different parts of the course support the development of the seven competences listed below? Look back through the course, making notes of the different topics that are relevant in each case.

Spend about half an hour working on this exercise. If you work through it in more detail as a way of starting your revision – with, say, a page for each competence – you will find that it is two or three hours well spent.

1 Plan, implement and review particular events, appeals and campaigns.

2 Communicate effectively with a variety of external and internal audiences.

3 Manage staff and volunteers.

4 Collect, analyse and manage relevant information.

5 Develop and maintain effective relations with donors, supporters and other relevant agencies.

6 Deal effectively with the commercial aspects of winning resources and support.

7 Choose and apply as appropriate various approaches or techniques for winning resources and support.

Here are some of the main points that come to mind about the seven competences.

1 Plan, implement and review particular events, appeals and campaigns.

A significant part of Book 1 is devoted to planning, a theme continued in Book 2's treatment of case and communications, and Book 3's guide to planning events. Books 4 and 6 look at the environment in which plans and strategies are made, and Books 2 and 5 outline evaluation.

2 Communicate effectively with a variety of external and internal audiences.

Practically the whole of Book 2 is relevant here, but other aspects of it occur in every other book too: the idea of events as theatre, and of dreaming up ideas for activities that reinforce or are consistent with your message; the discussion of 'making the ask', both face-to-face and at a distance, in Book 3; the discussion of preparing the ground, putting together an application or proposal, building support for your application and negotiating a deal in Book 4; not to mention your work online and exercises at tutorials and day schools.

3 Manage staff and volunteers.

Book 3 is the main one here, Book 4 emphasised the importance of good leadership and the sensitive coordination of the work of the teams involved in the pursuit of resources from other organisations. And the second session of Book 5 focuses on more general issues of people management.

4 Collect, analyse and manage relevant information.

Book 2 on managing media contacts. Book 3 on the importance of keeping good records in order to repeat and improve annual events, Book 5 on the uses of databases but also other, more mundane, aspects of information management. Book 4 on the need to keep all of your colleagues informed of your work. Book 5 on financial management, and Book 6's discussion of strategy based on scanning the environment for information.

5 Develop and maintain effective relations with donors, supporters and other relevant agencies

Knowing your supporters was a topic in Book 2. Roles and relationships in working with active supporters, understanding their motivations and donor development, were discussed in Book 3 which was all about cultivating relationships and drawing people in closer. Book 4 continued in the same vein about relationships with institutions.

6 Deal effectively with the commercial aspects of winning resources and support.

Commercial issues are discussed in Book 4. Book 3's discussion of charitable trading is also relevant, of course, as is the discussion of budgeting, costing and financial measures of performance in Book 5.

7 Choose and apply as appropriate various approaches or techniques for winning resources and support.

The discussion of planning in Book 1 is relevant here. This theme was continued in Book 2's discussion of planning for good public relations. Book 3's discussion of contribution multipliers, event management and volunteer support are also all relevant. Book 4 examined the importance of monitoring the progress of applications and building routine links with organisations, and in Book 5 the importance of regularly monitoring and reviewing activities in order to maintain and improve the performance of activities and events was emphasised. Book 6's strategic models based on the Ansoff Matrix and the GE Portfolio are also important here.

The previous activity will, we hope, have given you an opportunity to review your learning in the course themed around the seven broad competences which form its basis. This learning has been complemented by activities and assignments which have provided the opportunity to develop, reflect and assess your practice of these competences in your work. The next activity is about taking stock of how far you have come in this respect.

The competences around which this course was developed have been broadly specified in terms of their content and level of performance. As described here, 'competence' could be anywhere between a basic grasp of particular activities and what they involve, through to the ability to contribute significantly to such activities, and on to the ability to take the lead in the activity. This can be expressed in terms of three levels:

- the *awareness* level of competence – where you know a good deal about the activity but have little 'hands-on' experience
- the *contributory* level – where you can usefully join in, but lack the range of experience or the required underpinning knowledge and understanding to perform readily and independently in new circumstances
- the *initiating* level – where you have the depth of understanding and experience to initiate and take full responsibility for the activity.

With these different levels in mind, you can now chart your own professional development – looking back and looking forward.

ACTIVITY 3.3

For each of the seven competences, consider the following questions:

(a) Where were you when you started the course? (In order to answer this question, you might like to look back to Activity 1.12 in Book 1, where you answered a similar question.)

(b) Where are you now?

(c) What does your current job or voluntary position require?

(d) What do you expect your job or voluntary position will require in two to three years' time?

Answer in terms of the three levels of competence putting your answers into the chart below, using the letters A, C and I for *awareness*, *contributory* and *initiating* levels of competence.

Competences	Start	Now	Currently required	Required in future
1 Plan, implement and review particular events, appeals and campaigns.				
2 Communicate effectively with a variety of external and internal audiences.				
3 Manage staff and volunteers.				
4 Collect, analyse and manage relevant information.				
5 Develop and maintain effective relations with donors, supporters and other relevant agencies.				
6 Deal effectively with the commercial aspects of winning resources and support.				
7 Choose and apply as appropriate various approaches or techniques for winning resources and support.				

We will refer back to this chart later. For now, it is sufficient to note that, by considering what you have learned in this way, the focus shifts from the course content to your own professional development – which involves the integration of the knowledge, skills, techniques and understanding provided by the course, with practical, hands-on experience. A course like this is designed to underpin, consolidate, extend and speed up your 'learning by doing', but it needs to be complemented by direct, practical involvement.

3.3 BEYOND GOOD PRACTICE: JUDGEMENT, EXPERIENCE AND PERSONAL EFFECTIVENESS

If you look back, you will find that Book 1 listed eight areas of competence, not seven. So something is missing – and it is something important. The missing area of competence was described in terms of personal effectiveness, and it concerns attributes that are rather different from the skills and understanding that are required for the competences considered in Section 3.2.2. It is time to consider these personal qualities a little more closely – for they too have been another current running through the course.

For all the value of competence frameworks in specifying what needs to be done, the approach of breaking down competence into its constituent elements has its limitations. It makes it seem as though success is a matter of learning to do a series of discrete activities. The starting point, in terms of key roles, provides some protection against this but still the focus on separate elements can easily encourage a mechanistic, impersonal and fragmented view of professional development. Such a 'breaking-it-down' approach is too tidy and rational. It somehow loses the real complexity and challenge of work of this sort, and it ignores the extent to which how we set about our work reflects who we are and our different personal styles. Indeed, at its worst, this approach to management and professional development tends to reduce everything to a series of guidelines that are supposed to guarantee 'good practice'. To be sure, such guidelines can be useful – but seldom because they are being followed like the steps of a recipe in a cookery book. They set out what, in principle, should happen – but the real challenge is how to integrate and balance different aspects of your role. The key to being effective is judging what is appropriate in particular circumstances; you need to work out how much can realistically be carried out, and in what way, in the messy realities of, say, an organisation or a department that is being pulled in different directions and is feeling it has to run hard to stay in the same place.

So it is important that you keep a sense of proportion about the course and do not lose your nerve in the face of the avalanche of good-practice prescriptions that it has offered. Yes, of course, we all should plan more and better, for example – but, it has been said that life is what happens when you are busy making other plans. Indeed, the truth is that you cannot possibly do all the things that the course has told you to do all the time. However, having studied the course, you are now in a better position to judge what is *really* important – in *your* circumstances. Viewed in this way, winning resources and support is all about handling dilemmas and striking balances – rather than following recipes and guidelines.
So, experience and judgement are of the essence, along with other qualities that make for personal effectiveness.

ACTIVITY 3.4

The importance of a number of personal traits and qualities has been discussed at different points in the course. Make a list of the five that you consider are most important.

1 ______________________________

2 ______________________________

3 ______________________________

4 ______________________________

5 ______________________________

Personal qualities can be described in different ways. A possible list would include the following, which have all been discussed at one or more points in the course:

1. *Self-confidence, a willingness to put yourself on the line and the resilience to bounce back after the (inevitable) rejections (Books l, 3 and 4).*
2. *Creativity, flair and originality – in dreaming up new (and unique?) approaches and activities for fundraising and campaigning; in putting across your message, request or proposal; in developing your own professional style, hunches and 'sixth sense' of how to create the right circumstance for a little luck (Books 2, 3 and 4).*
3. *Enthusiasm and conviction for your cause (Books 2 and 3). See also point 8 below.*
4. *The capacity to cope with the inescapable dilemmas, ambiguities, and conflicting demands of fundraising and campaigning; coping with an unstructured and stressful job; working 'in the twilight zone' in your own organisation and at the interface between your own organisation and its environment (Books l, 3 and 4).*
5. *Tact, sensitivity and interpersonal skills; being good with people; being capable of reading a complex situation and thinking on your feet (Books 3, 4 and 5).*
6. *Being good with words and images – and being able to play to your own strengths as a communicator (Books 2 and 3).*
7. *Discretion; striking a balance between the personal and the impersonal, what is public and what is confidential information, consistent procedures and opportunism, informal networks and formal relationships (Books 1 and 4).*
8. *Detachment and a sense of what is feasible; being able to critically appraise proposals and performance; knowing when not to proceed with a planned activity or proposal (Books 3, 5 and 6).*

The problem with discussing the personal qualities that help in winning resources and support is that many people have trouble recognising themselves when described by a list of positive qualities. In addition, they wonder whether these are the sorts of qualities that you can develop or whether, instead, you are just born with them. The short answer is that they *can* all be developed – although some more readily and reliably than others. That said, it would be quite wrong to imagine that you have to develop all these qualities, let alone to a considerable degree. By far the most important personal quality of all is *knowing yourself.* An awareness of your own strengths and weaknesses allows you – through the collaboration that is fundamental to any effective organisation – to play to your strengths, compensate for your weaknesses and avoid situations in which your cause would be better served by someone else's contribution. Moreover, the great majority of people who gravitate towards the work of winning resources and support do so because, in some measure, they already have, or are quickly developing, many of the qualities that are needed. So the next exercise is as much about affirming your strengths as recognising your weaknesses.

ACTIVITY 3.5

How do you rate yourself with respect to the following personal qualities? For those that you consider problematic, write brief notes on how you can develop or support yourself. Alternatively, how can you arrange to have those qualities provided by others (for example, by drawing in other people or renegotiating your role in the organisation)?

Self-confidence

Creativity

Enthusiasm

Handling dilemmas

Interpersonal skills

Communication (verbal; visual)

Discretion

Detachment

Ability to delegate

It is always worth reminding yourself that you do not have to do everything!

3.4 WHAT NEXT?

A good course always raises as many questions as it answers. It sets a new agenda and does not just help you to tackle the old one. In this section we want to encourage you to think ahead to where you go next. Indeed, another way of pulling the course together is to reflect on the implications of the course for your organisation's and your own future development.

3.4.1 For your organisation

What are you going to do with your new ideas and understanding? In some ways, of course, you will have already been putting them to good use. But most people in most organisations cannot just do what they like: constraints of resources, policies, existing commitments, current practices and long-standing assumptions about 'the way we do things around here' all combine to limit the scope for new initiatives or to slow down the introduction of changes. This can be deeply frustrating, but it is not necessarily a bad thing. Your organisation's work is too important to be used as a testing ground for whatever bright idea someone picks up on a course (even if that someone is you and the course is this one). Besides, new ideas will only work if they are adopted by the people who have to carry them through and not just foisted on them. So changes have to be planned for, the case has to be made, and people have to understand and be involved.

So you need to consider the different ways in which you will contribute to the work of your organisation as a result of your greater understanding of how to win resources and support. Think about:

- the particular ideas you need to share with colleagues
- the specific initiatives that you can introduce to your part of the organisation
- the issues which the wider organisation needs to address, and for which your role, as internal persuader, is important.

ACTIVITY 3.6

Make lists of the points that come to mind under the three headings below. Then choose two or three points under each heading that you consider it is both *realistic* and *important* to tackle. Write notes on these, setting out how and when you can start to do what you think is needed.

(a) Sharing your learning with colleagues

(b) Specific initiatives in your area

(c) Issues to raise in the wider organisation

You can usefully end this sort of exercise by transferring the relevant points to your personal organiser or diary.

There are other things to bear in mind when considering how to introduce your own learning from this course into the work of your organisation. You may remember looking at the value of 'managing the expectations' of donors and supporters in Books 3 and 4. In a similar vein, you need to assist your own managers and colleagues to appreciate some of the complexities of defining 'effectiveness' and 'success' in fundraising and campaigning. If your own contribution to the work of the organisation is to be properly understood and developed, if your own performance is to be properly evaluated, then your managers and colleagues will need to explore many of the topics you considered in Book 5.

There may well be other key issues for you to explore, depending on the particular nature of your cause and your own position within the organisation. Your organisation may be rooted in very distinctive or deeply held values and beliefs; it may not readily command popular support; colleagues in other sections or departments will need to appreciate some of the problems you face and weigh up how your respective efforts can be mutually supportive and reinforcing. In all such situations, many of the wider judgements about what constitutes effectiveness, feasibility and success in winning resources and support will need to be shared.

3.4.2 For yourself

How will you continue your own professional development after this course? That may seem a strange question, but look back to Activity 3.3 and compare the levels of competence that you have now with those that are currently required, or that you expect will be required in two or three years' time. Wherever there is a gap, you need to consider what steps you can take to develop that particular competence. This could happen in many different ways:

- by arranging with your manager for the necessary work experience (for example, by joining a project team, or being seconded for a time to another department)

- by setting up an action-learning group with colleagues, or with others from your tutor group on this course (could you afford one evening a month, plus another evening of preparation?)
- through further reading, on your own, of books and articles on fundraising or of publications that are referenced in the course or elsewhere
- by subscribing to magazines or journals
- by networking through other organisations in your field or through conferences like the International Fundraising Workshop or the National Fundraising Convention
- by joining the Institute of Fundraising and seeking accreditation for the Certificate in Fundraising Management (CiFM) using successful completion of this course
- by joining other professional bodies such as the Council for Advancement and Support of Education (CASE), which is the professional body for fundraisers in education working with alumni and donors
- by taking other, more specialist, courses offered by either the OU Business School or another provider.

Your continuing professional development is your responsibility. By all means take a break for a few months – but you also need to think ahead so that you can recognise and create the opportunities you need.

ACTIVITY 3.7

Look back to Activity 3.3 and list all the competences, or aspects of competence, in which you believe that you need further development opportunities. Make notes on how you can set about developing further the competences you need or will need.

You should not lose sight of the fact that there is a competitive edge to winning resources and support. To be effective over the long term, you will need to 'stay ahead of the game'. You will need to be constantly alert, not just to new trends in the wider resource environment, but to the need to amend and extend your own style and approach. The formula which has worked well for several years may suddenly fail to secure the support you expect and you must be able to renew not just your methods but your thinking and practice too.

3.5 SUMMARY

Because this has been an activity-based session, its summary departs from the 'bullet-point' format of those used for the previous 22 sessions.

We hope that working through this session has helped you to appreciate the considerable ground you have covered since starting the course and to think about how you can carry on your own learning and development in the future. You may also feel a little overwhelmed – there are so many different concepts and techniques to learn. However, it is important not to get things out of perspective. Of course, what you have been learning will be useful, but it is just as important to keep the belief in and commitment to your cause, and the motivation and enthusiasm for what you are doing. If these shine through in your work, you are much more likely to win the support of others by your combination of knowledge, commitment and enthusiasm.

REFERENCES

Ansoff, H.I. (1987) *Corporate Strategy*, Harmondsworth, Penguin.

Brewster, R. (2007) 'Formulating an income strategy to fund the Mission', in Mordaunt, J. and Paton, R. (eds) (2007), pp. 199–212.

Bubb, S. (2002) 'Personal Trainer: I am told my organisation should have a mission statement. Why?' *Third Sector*, 20 November [online], http://www.thirdsector.co.uk/channels/Fundraising/Article/619663/PERSONAL-TRAINER-I-am-told-organisation-mission-statement-Why/ (Accessed 8 August 2007).

Burnett, K. (2002) *Relationship Fundraising* (2nd edn) San Francisco CA, Jossey Bass with the White Lion Press.

Dittrich, J.E. (1988) *The General Manager and Strategic Formulation*, Chichester, John Wiley and Sons.

Evans, E. and Saxton, J. (2003) Five key trends and their impact on the voluntary sector, London, nfp synergy [online], http://www.nfpsynergy.net/freereports (Accessed 20 October 2007).

Jump, P. (2007) 'Charities collaborate over shared HQ', *Third Sector*, 12 July [online], http://www.thirdsector.co.uk/News/Article/670758/Charities-collaborate-shared-HQ/ (Accessed 8 August 2007).

Kelly, A. (2003a) 'Income soars at Cancer Research', *Third Sector*, 5 February [online], http://www.thirdsector.co.uk/Channels/Fundraising/Article/618675/Income-soars-Cancer-Research/ (Accessed 8 August 2007).

Kelly, A. (2003b) 'Newsmaker: head of a popular cause – Peter Cardy, chief executive, Macmillan Cancer Relief', *Third Sector*, 16 July [online], http://www.thirdsector.co.uk/Channels/Fundraising/Article/615704/bNEWSMAKER-Head-popular-cause—Peter-Cardy-chief-executive-Macmillan-Cancer-Relief/ (Accessed 8 August 2007).

Little, M. (2003) 'News in Focus: Childrens Charities move towards shared projects', *Third Sector*, 2 April [online], http://www.thirdsector.co.uk/Channels/Fundraising/Article/618403/NEWS-FOCUS-children-aposs-charities-move-towards-shared projects.

Maggs, L. (2002) 'Street fundraiser goes bankrupt', *Third Sector*, 11 September [online], http://www.thirdsector.co.uk/Channels/Fundraising/Article/616580/bStreet-fundraiser-goes-bankrupt/ (Accessed 8 August 2007).

Mintzberg, H. (1987) 'The strategy concept I: five Ps for strategy', *California Management Review*, vol. 30, no. 1, pp. 11–24.

Mordaunt, J. and Paton, R. (eds) (2007) *Thoughtful Fundraising: Concepts, Issues and Perspectives*, London, Routledge/Milton Keynes, The Open University (Course Reader).

Mullin, R. (2002) *Fundraising Strategy* (2nd edn.), London, Charities Aid Foundation, Directory of Social Change and Institute of Fundraising.

Peacock, G. (2002) 'Opinion: a competitive streak doesn't suit this sector', Third *Sector*, 4 December [online], http://www.thirdsector.co.uk/Channels/Fundraising/Article/613425/bOPINION-competitive-streak-doesn-apost-suit-sector/ (Accessed 8 August 2007).

Peacock, G. (2003) 'Opinion: it's vital to view your work from donor's stance', *Third Sector*, 19 February [online], http://www.thirdsector.co.uk/Channels/Fundraising/Article/616098/OPINION-It-aposs-vital-view-work-donor-aposs-stance/ (Accessed 8 August 2007).

Shimmin, S. & Coles, G. (2007) *Campaigning in Collaboration*, London, National Council for Voluntary Organisations.

Stanford, P. (2003) 'Opinion: the core costs issue goes on', *Third Sector*, 19 March [online], http://www.thirdsector.co.uk/Channels/Fundraising/Article/622864/OPINION-core-costs-issue-goes/ (Accessed 8 August 2007).

Van der Gaag, N. (2007) 'Images in fundraising', in Mordaunt, J. and Paton, R. (eds) (2007) pp. 184–198.

ACKNOWLEDGEMENTS

Grateful acknowledgement is made to the following sources:

Figures

Figure 2.1: Ansoff, H. (1987) Corporate Strategy, Penguin Books Ltd;

Figure 2.2: Dittrich, J.E., (1988) The General Manager and Strategic Formulation, John Wiley and Sons, Inc;

Figure 2.3: Mintzberg, H. 'Deliberate and emergent strategies', California Management Review Vol. 30, No. 1, 1987, The Regents of the University of California;